IMPERMANEN

Midland & South Western Junction Railway

Part 1

Kevin Robertson
www.crecy.co.uk

First published in 2017 by Crécy Publishing

© Kevin Robertson 2017

ISBN 978 1 909328 56 3

A CIP record for this book is available from the British Library

Printed in England by LatimerTrend

www.crecy.co.uk

Front cover A unique survivor into the 21st century is the station and signal box at the former Savernake High Level. Located on the Marlborough to Grafton section of the MSWJ which opened on the 26th June 1898 it had but a limited life, the double line through here reduced to a single line with a goods loop on the north (down) side having the points controlled from the signal box albeit reduced in status to a ground frame from 1933. (It is possible the physical structure of the box here may even have been second-hand having previously been located at what was then referred to as Wolfhall Junction see: http://www.swindon-cricklade-railway.org/history.php#top). This cannot be confirmed but there are indeed similarities. It remained in this form until passenger services were 'temporarily' withdrawn in September 1958, a change that was made permanent in June 1959. On the same, latter, date 22nd June, the track of the former M & G railway was officially closed to all traffic from Marlborough to a point just south of where it had crossed over the GWR Berks & Hants line near Grafton South Junction. For reasons likely lost now in time, the station site survived for some time without trackwork but with the other physical structures basically intact. The former building was later converted into a private residence and the site is not open to the public.

Frontispiece Marlborough Low Level in the late 1950s. Eastleigh based 'U' class 2-6-0 No 31809 is at the head of three coaches bound for Savernake, Andover and Southampton on what was a typical MSWJ service from the final years. From the end of June 1958 there was just a single through passenger each way daily over the complete route from Cheltenham on through to Southampton, supplemented by a handful of Swindon to Marlborough or Savernake and Andover services. In the same year the three fitted through freight workings that had traversed the line were transferred away leaving just a local pick-up goods operating south of Cirencester. In the Colin Maggs book he refers to the railway creating an annual loss of £113,000 (approx £2.5m in 2017) and an average of just 89 passengers daily using Marlborough station out of which 64 were school children. An inevitable outcome was assured, it was just a question of how long away this would be. *Roger Holmes*

CONTENTS

INTRODUCTION: 'AGAINST THE GRAIN'

There is a risk sometimes in using a certain statement that although perfectly honest might be taken to be more of a cliché than truth. I have to accept that possibility when saying at the outset, the railway which forms the subject of this book is one I have wanted to write about for many years.

My friend Jeffery Grayer also surmised the Midland and South Western Junction Railway (along with the Somerset & Dorset, and Didcot, Newbury & Southampton routes) as running 'Against the Grain' and indeed I can think of no better introduction than this.

Each of the three lines mentioned does indeed run north south. In the west the S & D from Bath to Bournemouth, in the middle the MSWJ from Cheltenham to Southampton, and in the east the DNS from Didcot to Southampton. (For the purpose of this exercise it is convenient to ignore the fact that for each to reach their final destination they would all have to traverse metals that were well and truly owned by the London & South Western Railway.)

All three also served a specific traffic with the first two named having their reputations enhanced by operating their own locomotives and stock – for some years at least. Connecting lines, which is those not commencing or terminating in London can also serve a useful need, although in the rural communities through which each ran it would be through workings that would be needed in order to maintain finances rather than a reliance upon local, domestic traffic.

The north-south 'against the grain' route of the MSWJ. The line is shown at its peak but without reference to industrial lines nor specific sections of double/single line which, where relevant to the illustrations, are referred to in specific captions. *T B Sands*

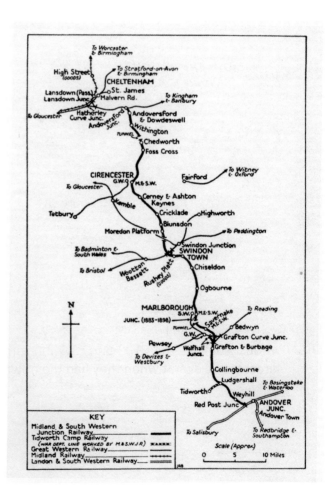

It was here that the Somerset and Dorset scored. Bournemouth and the Dorset coast was seen as a reliable destination for trippers and as such for decades the S & D was a railway with some through services on weekdays but which came alive at weekends and holidays with literally a nose to tail procession of trains from the north in the mornings and an equally considerable number of trains in the reverse direction at the end of the day. If the S&D had failings it was threefold. First the northern destination was at Bath where a reversal of direction was required for all services. Next the severe gradients especially north of Templecombe, and similarly the long stretches of single line. The last two factors meant operation was never easy. All would be a factor in the railways demise, the S&D destined also to be the last of three routes under discussion that retained a passenger service, until closure occurred in 1966.

Moving fully east, the Didcot, Newbury & Southampton managed to reach Winchester in 1885 but there the funds simply ran out and after six years as a terminus, there followed the ignominy of having to be bailed out by the LSWR in order for trains to reach Southampton at all. Like so many, the DNS had been born with grandiose ideas of becoming a through route, but more than a century later it is hard to understand how the directors could seriously believe the GWR and LSWR in turn would direct traffic over it when they had their own competing services. The independent DNS would struggle on until 1923, then becoming part of the GWR – as far as Winchester – and only really coming into its own for a brief timescale during WW2 when it formed one of the major supply routes to the south coast ports. As that doyen of researchers Tom Sands once described it, "The wartime traffic on the DNS was like a monster wave – quickly reaching its peak before falling away again never to be repeated." Without having its own locomotives and rolling stock, the little railway never quite ascribed to the charisma of its westward counterparts although it did have its own loyal following (the present writer included), until the inevitable end came. Indeed it remains a sad wonder how it managed to survive at all, albeit by that time just with freight, until the summer of 1964.

In the middle of both of these was the Midland & South Western Railway. Born out of the 1884 amalgam of the Swindon, Marlborough and Andover, and the Swindon and Cheltenham Extension, companies. Here was a railway which from the outset was a thorn in the flesh of the mighty Great Western. This book though is not a place for politics nor a full detailed history of those troubled times, suffice to say such history is more than able described in those volumes referred to in the biography, notable those by (in alphabetical order), Mike Barnsley, David Batholemew, and Colin Maggs.

Swindon was of course for decades regarded as the epicentre of the GWR, and to have a competitor passing through it was anathema. Suffice to say life was not easy for the MSWJ, Paddington (in this context meaning the headquarters of the GWR) doing all it could to disrupt the operation and indeed expansion of the line. So much so that only a few years later the arrangement of running powers for the SMA over the GWR's Marlborough branch from Marlborough to Savernake became so difficult as to cause the building of a separate railway between these points so enabling what was by then the

A unique survivor, this former MSWJ locomotive tender was photographed in the early 1960s, corroded yes, but with its original owner's crest still showing through and somewhat better than the words 'Great Western' which had likely been applied in 1923. Careful study reveals it has probably been in use as something akin to a sludge carrier, the centre wheelset removed and an outlet valve added. Sadly this was before the railway preservation movement had got into its stride and this valuable relic was destined to be broken up. The late R C 'Dick' Riley, recounted a story he had heard that upon takeover by the GWR the foreman at the former MSWJ works at Cirencester – for a short time still involved in maintaining and repairing locomotives – send a request to Swindon for what he considered to be the requisite amount of paint necessary for a particular locomotive. Back came considerably less than the applied for amount. Perhaps MSWJ standards were higher, perhaps they might even have been regarded by Swindon as excessive, but considering the MSWJ livery and crest would have been applied at Cirencester pre-1923 and the wording 'Great Western' sometime post 1923 and yet it is the latter that has faded worse, seemingly the Cirencester man was indeed right in the first place.

MSWJ to bypass these difficulties altogether and giving rise to one of several (throughout the country that is) duplicate routes the origins of which may be blamed entirely upon railway politics.

The GWR though would have its revenge, for in 1923 the independent MSWJ was forcibly absorbed into the folds of the Great Western, although financial disagreements meant this did not actually fully take place until September 1923, nine months later than intended. After this it was for its remaining life a cross-country GWR route, usually limited in traffic to what was available from the community through which it passed and with some, although limited, through carriage workings. Like the DNS too, it would find a role in WW2, traffic for the south coast directed over it, but also like the DNS by the 1950s it was becoming ever more difficult to justify the retention of a long and let us be honest, unprofitable railway. What through workings there were easily diverted to be accommodated on other lines.

The MSWJ had also the melancholy distinction of being the first major closure successfully (the word was hardly successful other than to the accountants) undertaken by the then Western Region although it would not be long before many others would follow in quick succession. This occurred in 1961, sections of the line being closed completely and meaning it was not longer available as a through route for freight although traffic to Moredon, from Swindon, to Swindon Town from Swindon Junction, to Marlborough from Savernake, and to Ludgershall / Tidworth from Andover, would continue. At the time of writing that from Andover as far as Ludgershall is still in situ at least but one must question its long term future.

The locomotive and rolling stock of the MSWJ suffered mixed fortunes post 1923. To be fair the standardisation policies of the GWR meant much was considered redundant at the outset although some rolling stock did survive for some time at least, likely as not as there was simply not the available standard stock to replace it immediately. The locomotives too had a mixed fate although again this not be repeated here as it is well covered in the Mike Barnsley books. Suffice to say the best known survivors were three 2-4-0 tender engines built by Messrs Dubs in 1894 and which became GWR Nos 1334-6. All entered British Railways service in 1948, with the last of this remarkable trio surviving until 1954. Examples will be seen in the text but this is also how they only survive as sadly all went for scrap.

Between 1961 and the present day, population increase has seen development banish many signs of the railway perhaps most especially in the area of Swindon and Cirencester. Road development has also dissected across the trackbed most noticeably with the M4 which cuts across the former route of the railway south of Swindon and also involving the A417/419 at Cirencester. Elsewhere bridges have been removed, saving maintenance or to recycle valuable metals, some stations have been converted in residences, or trackbed restored to agricultural use.

But whilst the physical signs of the railway may be slowly disappearing year on year, its history is forever fixed and cannot be ignored. Despite the popularist clamour for railway reopenings in recent years, it is unlikely the MSWJ route will ever see traffic again. In many ways that is sad, for congestion on some roads, notably the A345 south of Swindon

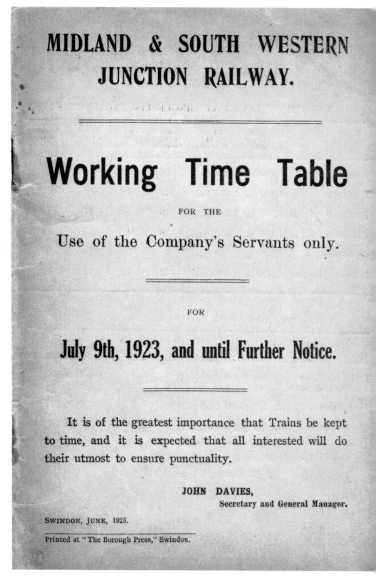

MIDLAND & SOUTH WESTERN JUNCTION RAILWAY.

Working Time Table

FOR THE

Use of the Company's Servants only.

FOR

July 9th, 1923, and until Further Notice.

It is of the greatest importance that Trains be kept to time, and it is expected that all interested will do their utmost to ensure punctuality.

JOHN DAVIES,
Secretary and General Manager.

SWINDON, JUNE, 1923.

Printed at " The Borough Press," Swindon.

means that if an alternative were available it would surely find a use. But then it is far easier to upgrade an existing road than to build/rebuilt a new railway alongside.

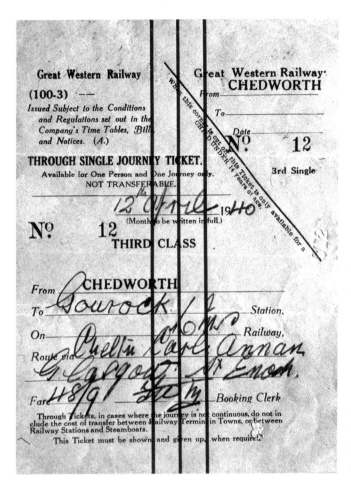

As set out I intended the work to fit neatly into the, albeit enlarged 'Impermanent Way *Special*' series. I was wrong. Having edited hundreds of books I now know how the author must have felt when told, 'Sorry, you have just got too much material'. Consequently having compiled in excess of 260 captions (instead of the specified 140) it was with some trepidation that I approached Jeremy at Crecy with a request to split the work into two. I am grateful for him agreeing and so showing trust in the project. This then is 'Book 1' taking the story of the MSWJ as far as the final weekend, 9/10th September 1961. What followed after this will feature in 'Part 2'.

The intention of this combined work is not to rewrite or repeat (too much) history. Instead it is to take a fresh look at a charismatic railway using material much of which – we hope – will be new to the printed page although to illustrate certain points some duplication cannot be avoided. In other works, previous authors have concentrated on perhaps the stations, locomotives, or line history all valuable subjects of course. This time the general onus is on the very last years – with a few flashbacks - and the time post-closure although I would still certainly comment the present reader to read the Tom Sands, Mike Barnsley, David Barthomew, and Colin Maggs works on the line. Fifty-five plus years have now passed since a train ran the length of the railway and so this volume may legitimately been deemed to be unashamed 'nostalgia'. At the same time it is as was said earlier, to fulfil an ambition of the present author and to share with others a love for a railway which I still mourn but regret I never witnessed during its operational life.

Kevin Robertson

ACKNOWLEDGEMENTS

The compilation of this book would not have been possible without the generous help of Neil Lover. Neil hosts the truly excellent www.swindonsotherrailway.co.uk website which I can heartily recommend to anyone with an interest in the line. It does however come with a warning – I consider a few minutes would be enough to view the various images and pages.......*four hours plus later I was disturbed by a shout from elsewhere, "Are you ever coming down...?"* . A wonderful way indeed to spend (certainly not waste) some time. Thanks are also due to the numerous individuals from the website who have allowed their material and knowledge to be reproduced in these pages. I must also thanks friends, Mike Barnsley, Sean Bolan, Alan Butcher, Amyas Crump, David Hyde who at short notice kindly agreed to read through the text, Gerry Nichols, and Stephen Duffell, (*nearly*) all Great Western enthusiasts through and through and who have also been generous with their advice and respective contributions. Indeed the book was I thought perhaps 90% complete when I happened to speak to Stephen and a few days later a disc with almost 100 images appeared! Finally to Jeff Grayer, whose original idea it had been to produce a book entitled 'Against the Grain'* and who I will admit I am responsible for talking out of some years ago. Please believe me if I say that at that time it was done with the best intentions and certainly not so I might steal the idea for myself later! All unaccredited photo images come from private photograph collections and with nothing written on the reverse to indicate their provenance. To anyone who I might also have forgotten (I use the excuse of age), my thanks and also apologies.

* Both Tom Sands and later Colin Maggs used the similar 'Across the Grain' reference in their respective works.

SELECTED BIBLIOGRAPHY

'Gone with Regret', George Behrend. Published Jersey Artists 1964.

'Industrial Locomotives of Central Southern England', Roger Hateley. Industrial Railway Society.

'The Midland and South Western Junction Railway', Colin Maggs. Published David & Charles 1967.

'The Midland and South Western Junction Railway', T B Sands. Published Oakwood Press 1959.

'The Midland and South Western Junction Railway, Vol 1', David Bartholomew Mike Barnsley. Wild Swan Publications 1982.

'The Midland and South Western Junction Railway, Vol 2 Locomotives', Mike Barnsley. Wild Swan Publications 1991.

'The Midland and South Western Junction Railway, Vol 3 Carriages and Wagons', Locomotives'. Mike Barnsley. Wild Swan Publications 1995.

'Impermanent Ways Vol 3 Wiltshire', Jeffrey Grayer. Noodle Books 2012.

'Rails Across the Plain: The Amesbury – Bulford Railway', Jeffery Grayer, Noodle Books, 2011.

'Track Layout Diagrams of the GWR and BRWR, Section 22: Midland and SWJCN' R A Cooke.

'The Marlborough Branch', Kevin Robertson and David Abbott. Irwell Press 1990.

'The Old Photographs series; The Midland & South Western Junction Railway', Brian Bridgeman and Mike Barnsley Chalford Publishing Co 1994.

Also referred to: timetables public and working.

ABBREVIATIONS

A&R – Andover and Redbridge Railway.

B&C – Banbury and Cheltenham Railway.

B&H – Berks and Hants Railway.

B&HER – Berks and Hants Extension Railway.

DEMU – Diesel-Electric multiple unit.

DNS – Didcot, Newbury & Southampton Railway.

ESM – Economic System of Maintenance.

GWR – Great Western Railway.

LSWR – London and South Western Railway.

MESM – Motor Economic System of Maintenance.

Mid.R – Midland Railway.

MRly – Marlborough Railway.

M&G – Marlborough and Grafton Railway.

PT – Pannier Tank.

RCH – Railway Clearing House

SCE – Swindon and Cheltenham Extension Railway.

SMA – Swindon, Marlborough and Andover Railway.

S&D – Somerset and Dorset Railway.

Note – The generic word 'token' has been used to refer to single line working in the text. This should be seen as referring to 'tablet, staff, or token' types, all of which effect the same result.

PART 1 - SETTING THE SCENE

Building of the Swindon and Cheltenham Extension Railway near Chedworth in 1888/89. Construction of the railway north of Swindon was to be protracted, dogged by difficulties both financial and geographical and it was not to be until 1st August 1891 that through traffic working from Southampton was possible. Even then there were difficulties, notably between Savernake and Marlborough as is discussed later. What we see here is the embryonic railway not far from the Chedworth Roman Villa. The locomotive seen here may well be an 0-4-0ST and appropriately named 'Chedworth'. If so it belonged to Messrs Charles Braddock who had taken over the contract for construction from Messrs, Watson, Smith and Watson which firm had been released from their contract in November 1884 and subsequently went bankrupt in 1885. It is believed 'Chedworth' was one of five small locomotives used in the construction. (It was also the practice of contractors to name locomotives after locations or dignitaries associated with the work they were engaged upon.) Seventy years then separates this image and that on the opposite page. Seventy years – less than a lifetime to many – which decades would see the MSWJ rise from obscurity to a peak before slowly sinking back again towards obscurity. The same time span is small when compared with the lifespan of some routes, less than twice that amount for the Great Western main line for example and so we must question was the investment in time, effort, and finance in building the MSWJ even pointless? At the time no, although when compared against the requirements of today the answer would have to be yes. But during those 70 years of operation the railway afforded employment, transport, and service. Those who lost out were the financial backers whose investment may still be seen buried in the earthworks that remain. Arguably too it is the present generation who have equally poor by not attempting to make use of what remnants remain, but perhaps we have in the form of cycle and foot paths, road schemes and not forgetting of course the present day heritage Swindon & Cricklade Railway, none of which would have existed had the trackbed not have been available in the first place.

No 31801 leaving South Cerney on its way towards Cricklade, Swindon and beyond, 5th August 1961. Seen is the southern end of the station loop which had been extended by 132 yards in 1942. The fireman has some decent coal available to him whilst the use of a LM Region coach is perhaps a little unusual.*Mark B Warburton courtesy Mrs Margaret Warburton.*

PART 2A - THE ORIGINAL RAILWAY CHELTENHAM TO SAVERNAKE

Taking the GWR line east, the railway climbed and passed Cheltenham South and Leckhampton, and also Charlton Kings station before arriving at Andoversford. As opened in 1891, the SCE were not allowed to stop their trains

Below and right **General Railway Clearing House diagrams for the MSWJ dated 1922. Services over the line commenced at the Midland Railway station of Cheltenham Lansdown and where the MSWJ and MR maintained cordial relations. Leaving Cheltenham southbound, services traversed via a junction with the GWR to join the latter's route west in the direction of Kingham and Banbury.**

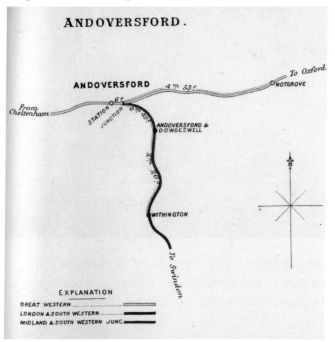

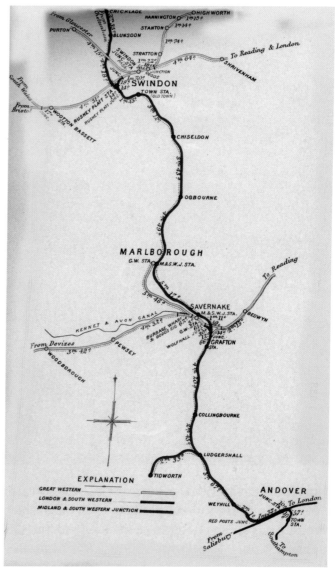

at the GWR Andoversford site which meant a station named Andoversford & Dowdeswell was provided approximately half a mile south of the GWR location but on the MSWJ proper. This arrangement persisted until 1904.

Continuing south the railway passed Withington and then in order (although not shown on the RCH maps), the stations of Chedworth, Foss Cross, Cirencester and Cerney & Ashton Keynes. Cirencester was the main works and locomotive depot of the MSWJ, although at various times there were also other smaller depots at Chedworth, Swindon, a temporary shed at Grafton & Burbage, Ludgershall, Tidworth, and Andover. Referring now to the second map, the railway again continued south through Cricklade and Blunsden to reach Swindon. To avoid confusion with the existing GWR branch terminus at Cirencester – reached from Kemble – Cirencester (MSWJ) had the suffix 'Watermoor' added to the name after 1st July 1924, the branch terminus at Cirencester thence being referred to as 'Town'. There was never any physical rail connection between the two Cirencester stations. In the same way there might otherwise have been confusion at Swindon, that on the GWR main line was referred to as 'Swindon Junction' whilst the MSWJ site was 'Swindon Town', a reference to its location in the Old Town district of Swindon.

On through Wiltshire, there were stations at Chiseldon and then Ogbourne before Marlborough was reached. The SMA reached Marlborough in July 1881 and which was for the next two years a dead end terminus. Then in February 1883 a connection was provided with the existing GWR Marlborough branch although each company maintained their own station each also having the straightforward name 'Marlborough' - as if wishing to ignore the presence of the other. From 1883 until 1898 MSWJ trains used the steeply graded GWR line to reach Savernake before turning south on to their own metals again at Wolfhall Junction. (For a history just of the GWR Marlborough branch see reference in the bibliography.)

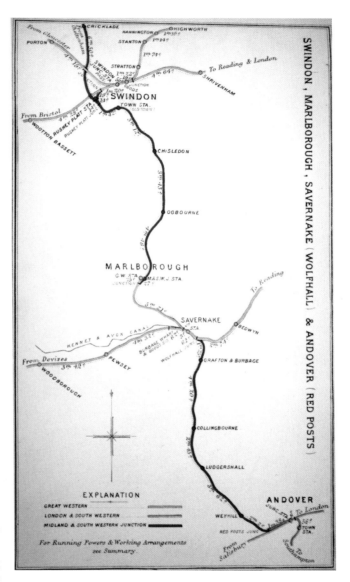

Here we have a variation on the standard RCH diagrams with this pre 1898 RCH diagram showing the railway terminating at Marlborough and starting again east of Savernake.

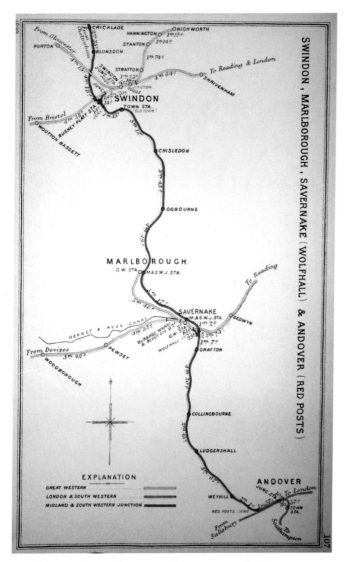

In this next diagram which is post 1898, the Marlborough and Grafton line is included.

South of this point the SMA had from 1st May 1882 no choice but to terminate their trains at a temporary terminus at Grafton station, running a shuttle between

this point and Andover -temporarily with the last few miles over LSWR metals until their own indepent and parallel line was ready. Fortunately relations with the LSWR were far better than those with the GWR! From Grafton on, there were stopping places at Collingbourne, Ludgershall and Weyhill before Andover (Junction) was reached. Andover Town station, approximately 1,250 yards south east of 'Junction' was on the LSWR 'Andover to Redbridge' railway (via Romsey of course) and which would become the regular means of access for MSWJ trains to Southampton very soon afterwards.

Away from the 'main line' we must of course mention the Tidworth branch, funded by and opened for the benefit of the War Department in July 1901 and for public goods and passengers in July and October 1902 respectively. This formed a facing connection with the up line just after the north end of Ludgershall station. There were no intermediate stopping places on the Tidworth branch although as might be expected there were extensive sidings at the terminus as well as a line continuing into Lucknow barracks. The Tidworth line eventually passed into GWR ownership in the late 1920s but reverted again to military control post 1955.

Elsewhere there had been sidings and a timber loading bank between Withington and Chedworth, some ballast sidings south of Chedworth, and the same south of Withington. South of Foss Cross the 'Foss Cross Lime & Limestone Quarry Co' had their own sidings. South of Blunsden a single platform was provided in 1895 principally for milk but which passengers might also use. Beyond this came Moredon milk platform this time exclusively for goods use. In the same area in 1928 came an extensive group of sidings serving what was Swindon Corporation Electricity Works, along with the service to Ludgershall, these sidings saw some of the last services, albeit freight, to use a part of the former MSWJ.

At Rushey Platt a connection was made between the GWR and MSWJ to enable trains to run between the two Swindon stations. The MSWJ crossed the GWR on a metal bridge whilst the physical connection was such that trains left Swindon Junction (GWR) and proceeded west before turning south west through 90° to join the MSWJ facing Swindon Town. Because of the difference in heights between the two lines this was also a steep climb. But oh that it might be so simple, as again railway politics came into play, this time meaning the GWR were in no hurry to complete the physical connection between the two lines at Rushey Platt. Consequently at first the SMA literally ending in what was then a field although trains did start using the actual junction in early 1882. Meanwhile the SCE was progressing northwards and as a result it was not long before Rushey Platt would boast four platform faces – two each for the link to the GWR and for the SCE – making this stopping place for a short time at least the stopping place with the greatest number of platforms on the MSWJ system! Largest it may have been but likely quietest so far as traffic was concerned. Indeed in what was then such a rural environment traffic could never be expected to be great and passenger services were destined to be withdrawn as early as 1905 although milk continued to be handled.

South of Swindon, Chiseldon had once had a branch south and west of the station to Draycott Military camp whilst south of Ogbourne was a small siding to a horse dock at Ogbourne St Andrew.

The situation between Marlborough and Savernake was not perhaps as complicated as has sometimes been made out. As mentioned, originally the SMA used a connection with the GWR Marlborough branch but then in 1898 opened its own independent line to bypass this. From this time until 1923 the situation was that each company had its own route between Marlborough and Savernake but with no interchange at Marlborough – the 1883 connection between the MSWJ and GWR having been removed. This was reinstated in 1926 but the big change came in 1933 when the GWR closed most of their own line leaving the former GWR station at Marlborough to handle goods alone. At the same time at the Savernake

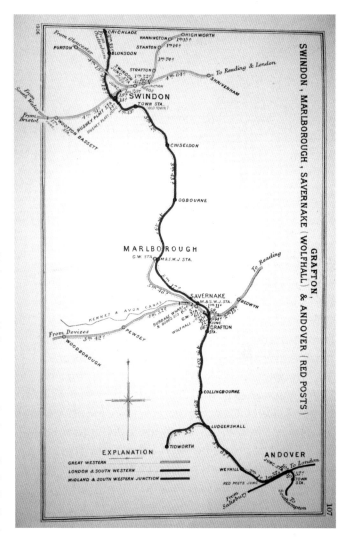

Finally post 1905, the Tidworth branch is included. This was the final extent of the MSWJ and no further expansion so far as route mileage took place although various schemes were put forward principally by the military to connect Tidworth with the railway at Bulford.

MSWJ 009 – A contemporary coloured postcard from Edwardian times showing Swindon Town station c1904/5. The view is looking south with the line curving past the commodious goods shed before continuing south towards Andover. Unfortunately it has not been possible to identify the locomotive or working with any accuracy. The wagons on the right show a dominance of LSWR ownership, nothing unusual in that as under Railway Clearing House agreements various types were known as 'common user' and might in theory therefore be seen anywhere. This policy avoided goods having to be 'trans-shipped' between vehicles at company boundaries.

end, the original GWR line was connected to the former up line of the M&G and meaning from Marlborough southwards, the former double track of the M&G was now operated as two single lines, one continuing on to Savernake High Level (named as such in July 1924 - the former M&G/MSWJ) station, and the other going to the GWR station at Savernake (renamed Low Level in July 1924). Trains on the former MSWJ line could thus use either route between Savernake and Marlborough.

The other side of Savernake the connection from the GWR at Wolfhall Junction had existed or not according to politics and/or date. Suffice to say that post 1900 this connection was permanently available, although initial just for wagon transfers.

In 1905 access to the Ludgershall – and thence Tidworth – was made somewhat easier for GWR services heading west by the provision of a chord linking the B&H with the MSWJ east of Wolfhall Junction. Likely used primarily for military and/or excursion traffic, this survived until 1957. It is not believed there was any regular timetabled services over this chord.

Another industrial line diverged from the main line at Grafton. This ran to Dodsdown brickworks and was in operation from 1903 to just 1910 its output destined for the building of the Tidworth barracks. Finally a new halt was provided by the GWR at Collingbourne Kingston in 1933 - between the stations at Grafton and Collingbourne proper.

The end of the MSWJ was signified at Red Post Junction west of Andover – so called according to folklore as a red post was located here as a marker. Originally a physical junction with the LSWR the MSWJ later had its own independent line running alongside the MSWJ whilst the junction was later doubled before finally reverting again to single line in its final years.

With much written already on the MSWJ the decision had be how to present this look at the line in a new light. Fortunately that was made easy with the choice of colour material available – not all there is by any means – as a trawl through the internet will reveal additional views available through commercial and other sources. But even if all this were collated together there would still be gaps and in consequence the decision was made to make an initial pictorial journey down the line using colour wherever possible.

On 18th December 1925, Edward Wallis recorded this view of Cheltenham Lansdown station with GWR and LMS trains awaiting departure. To the left is a GWR 'Duke' (likely No 3290 'Severn') on a Southampton bound train whilst that to the right is an LMS service likely bound for Gloucester and Bristol. *Edward Wallis*

Above **The locomotive shed at Cheltenham High Street where MSWJ and later GWR engines were serviced where necessary. On the left is another 'Duke' with an MSWJ 4-4-0 on the adjacent road but stood further back.** *LGRP*

Left **The other side of Lansdown Junction with the GWR/MR route to Gloucester continuing straight ahead and that to Andoversford (and eventually Banbury) on the left, this latter route had been doubled in 1902 to accommodate additional traffic on the MSWJ. The trap points on the 'branch' were necessary due to the steep gradient heading east and were intended to catch any runaways before they reached the main line. On the left the distinctive building is part of Dean Close school.** *Edward Wallis*

Andoversford station looking west with the original station signal box visible – the replacement structure seen in the next view was position a few yards off the end of the platform on the same side. The distance between the west end of the station and the junction meant it was too far for the single signal box to control the MSWJ junction hence the requirement for a second structure at what was Andoversford Junction.

The replacement station signal box at Andoversford at the west end of the site. Dating from 1935, it worked with Charlton Kings to the west (towards Cheltenham) and Andoversford Junction to the east - where the MSWJ diverged. The signal box outlived the MSWJ by just over a year and was closed on 15th October 1962.

The former Andoversford and Dowdeswell station which closed in 1927. This is looking up towards
Andoversford proper with the A40 main road running out of sight to the right of the stone wall.
The SCE railway was originally single track from Andoversford (GWR) south with passing loops at
the stations but the route had been doubled as far south as Cirencester by mid 1902. No doubt for
reasons of economy the same section was singled by the Great Western in July 1928. What is perhaps
surprising is that a reversion to double track did not take place in WW2 recourse instead being made
to extended loops in places. The view here is post 1928 with the main line now operating on the
right hand track only and that to the left classified as a siding. After it became redundant as a railway
station, the main building alongside the A40 was used as a transport café.

Right **Mention has already been made of the fact that the MSWJ owned and operated its own locomotives. Some examples of these will be seen at various stages throughout this work but as a taster here is No 20, an 0-6-0 built by Beyer Peacock in 1899 and one of six identical engines from this batch. The engine is running tender-first towards Andoversford (GWR) heading north on 10th August 1921. The storm sheet between engine and tender would give the crew some protection against inclement weather when running this way but at the obvious expense of visibility. According to David Bartholomew, the train may well have shunted the timber siding at Chedworth Woods. The first wagon may also be seen to be displaying MSWJ initials.** *Roger Carpenter*

Right **On a grey April day in April 1961, it is the turn of No 31626 to be in charge of the 7.50 am Andover Junction to Cheltenham service. The train was recorded on the final section of single track before Andoversford is reached.** *G T Robinson / Amyas Crump collection*

Taken from the final working time table for the MSWJ, dated '9th July 1923 and until Further Notice'.

FOR THE INFORMATION OF THE COMPANY'S SERVANTS ONLY.

SHUNTING AT FOSS CROSS.

Whenever it is necessary to shunt wagons from the Sidings to the Main Line at Foss Cross Station, the engine or brake van must be at the Cirencester end of such wagons to prevent their running away towards Cirencester.

TRAINS CROSSING AT SINGLE LINE STATIONS.

When Trains cross each other at Single Line Stations, the Signalman on duty must ascertain by personal observation—

I. That each train has arrived complete with tail lamps affixed, and

II. That all the vehicles on each train are standing well clear of the adjoining loop line before the points are reversed, and the signals lowered for the departure of the trains from the Station.

WORKING OF GOODS' TRAINS BETWEEN ANDOVERSFORD JUNCTION AND CHELTENHAM.

All Goods Trains running towards Cheltenham must stop dead at the stop board on the top of the Andoversford Bank.

Before starting again, the Guard on those trains which consist of more vehicles than the Engine and Van, must put down sufficient wagon brakes nearest the engine. The train must then be started very quietly and slowly drawn on to the steep falling gradient, and as it is thus being drawn the Guard must continue putting brakes down until the whole of the vehicles are on the incline. When the Driver feels by the movement and weight of the train that there are enough brakes down, he must give two short sharp whistles to indicate that he is satisfied that sufficient brake power is in operation to properly control the train, and to stop it at any point on the steepest part of the incline should it be necessary to do so, but the Guard will be held jointly responsible with the Driver for working the train safely down the incline.

The Engine Driver must always use steam to pull the whole train on to the incline, in order to be thoroughly satisfied that a sufficient number of wagon brakes have been applied, and he must not give the two whistles referred to above until the whole of the train has been drawn on to the incline.

The Engine and Van Brakes must in all cases be off when the train is started, so that these brakes may be held in reserve and ready for use to steady the train, or to stop it at any point on the steepest part of the incline, should it be necessary to do so

The Guard must closely watch the train while descending the incline and if necessary must assist the Driver by every means in his power to keep the train under proper control.

REFERENCES.

C.R.—Call if required.   B.—Class B Goods.   R.R.—Runs if required.

*Stops to shunt for other trains.   X—One train crosses another on Single Line.

Speed through Ludgershall, Marlborough, Swindon Town and Rushey Platt Stations must not exceed 20 miles per hour.

Speed through Andoversford Junction must not exceed 10 miles per hour.

Speed of Coaching Stock Trains must not exceed 40 miles per hour, and Goods Trains 35 miles per hour, between Dowdeswell and Cirencester, on the Down Line.

(1)

Right **GWR No 1011 – ex MSWJ No 27 of 1902 entering Withington on a Cheltenham working on 11th September 1935, coincidentally 26 years to the day before passenger services ceased operation. The engine has been through Swindon works and received a taper boiler in which form it would survive until May 1937. Of note is the three coach passenger load, typical of local workings on the line during the inter-war period. The exception to this might be when a horse box or two were added.** *LGRP*

Right **Chedworth station basking in the sun on 7th August 1961. The up line had been removed from here in 1928 and in the ensuing years the unused platform has gone the same way. Just north of the site by the overbridge was a stone retaining wall. At this point in time with only a matter of weeks before closure no one is going to come around to effect a repaint but which looks desperately overdue. Goods were never handled here, freight instead being directed to and consigned to Foss Cross. The GWR did propose freight facilities be provided but the plan was never implemented. Notwithstanding the state of the building, the permanent way looks in fine fettle: bull-head track on three-bolt chairs affixed to concrete sleepers.** *Mark B Warburton courtesy Mrs Margaret Warburton.*

Left A fascinating view of the ballast quarry north of Foss Cross which was used to supply all the ballast requirements for the MSWJ. On the raised portion of track a small steam locomotive is standing and with a goodly amount of coal for it on the wooden trestle at lower level, possibly the engine carried the name 'Beacon'. The main line is that running on the extreme right. Somewhat unusual is the fact that the facing point off the main line does not have a facing point lock as this was a requirement for facing connections off of passenger lines. The sidings here were still in place although certainly disused for their original purpose post 1923, instead for a time after this they were used as one of the storage locations for coaching stock inherited from the various lines that had been absorbed by the GWR in 1923. *Corinthian Museum*

Left In the same way that the section south of Swindon to Marlborough across the Wiltshire Downs might well be regarded as somewhat exposed, so might the line in the vicinity of Foss Cross. Here the winds might whip across to catch the unwary, indeed it was commonly regarded as the coldest station on the railway although on this day, in August 1961, all appears calm – for the present at least. Another Eastleigh based engine, 'U' No 31818 has arrived from Cheltenham on what was then the only through train of the day. *Mark B Warburton courtesy Mrs Margaret Warburton*

Right One of the last images of Cirencester (MSWJ) Watermoor with running lines through both platforms, taken by Mark Warburton on 14th May 1960. The train is Southampton bound with No 31804 in charge. Notice the first two vehicles are Hawkesworth stock, likely no more than ten years old but already cascaded on to secondary routes in consequence of the mass introduction of BR Standard Mk 1 vehicles. Cirencester would ends its days with just one through set of rails, the down line, this was in consequence of the underline bridge at the north end of the station being hit by a digger which rendered that part of the bridge unsafe. The up line was then placed out of use in the spring of 1960 and formally 'taken out of use' in November of the same year. It was lifted in January 1961. In consequence the signal box was closed in August 1960 with the yard accessed by ground frames unlocked by the token on a lengthened single line section running from Foss Cross to South Cerney.
Mark B Warburton courtesy Mrs Margaret Warburton

Right Recorded by signal engineer Edward Wallis, this is Cirencester at an unknown date but likely in the late 1920s. The single line token set down and pick up posts appear freshly painted - the set down post was always the first one – and as these are provided for both up and down trains it must be after July 1928 when the line north of Cirencester reverted to single track. On the left is the station goods shed built of brick whilst the main station building and base to the water tower were of local Cotswold stone. (The locomotive works was further to the left and will be referred to later.) The structure of the tall signal box was supplied by the Gloucester Carriage and Wagon Company and in 1923 was reported as containing 19 levers.

The Act of Parliament for the SCE in 1881 also authorised two additional lines that were never built. One of these was a north curve that would have allowed southbound 'MSWJ' trains to join the GW main line heading towards Swindon - likely to have been called something akin to 'Rushey Platt North'. The second line would have been a route from Cirencester to Fairford. For its part Fairford would forever be the terminus of a long branch line from Oxford. But public transport between Cirencester to Fairford did not have to be restricted to rail travel of course, and from March 1898 until late 1899 an enterprising individual established an oil fired steam driven 'road motor' to operate between the two. The front portion was similar to a 'Foden' steam lorry and contained the driver plus accommodation for goods and parcels, the rear a covered passenger trailer having accommodation, it is believed, for 18 persons although it is reported that at times passengers might be required to transfer to the enclosed front portion to improve adhesion. The experience of same however on solid wheels allied to the conditions of the roads at the time are perhaps best left to the imagination. It was also a private enterprise venture with no known business connection with the railway. Taken from a poor newspaper cutting the vehicle is shown here.

We come now to South Cerney (Cerney and Ashton Keynes until July 1924). Here a platform for down trains together with a small signal box for controlling the workings was added in 1900. The loop was extended at the south end to allow for wartime traffic in 1942 and a replacement signal box provided. Slightly surprising is that this replacement structure – seen in the image above – was to a standard GWR pre-war design rather the stark 'ARP' type boxes that were being built co-terminus with the similar improvements taking place on the neighbouring DNS line. Wartime needs though were long in the past in August 1960 when Mark Warburton captured No 30801 arriving at the station from the north with a three coach train of Midland stock likely bound for Southampton. As at Foss Cross, no platform canopy was provided. *Mark B Warburton courtesy Mrs Margaret Warburton*

We now have a small selection taken on the same day at Cricklade, and in the final years of the line the last stopping place before reaching Swindon. Cricklade had originally been an important station for goods which was reflected in the original siding accommodation which included a commodious goods shed and expansive cattle dock and loading platform. Whilst this traffic slowly fell away over the decades, the station reached its peak so far as track was concerned in July 1942 when the station loop was extended at the north end. Unlike at South Cerney however, the original signal box was deemed suitable to retain and is seen in one of the photographs with its 'greenhouse' extension. (Originally all timber, at some time the original timber base has been superseded with a brick base.) The first view is of 'U' class 2-6-0 No 31804 arriving southbound, the coaching stock all former GWR/WR vehicles. In the second view the train has arrived and is awaiting departure. Lack of passengers, as is woefully apparent in so many of the images showing the regular service, could lead to long waits at the intermediate stations with no necessity to load quantities of parcels as might have been the case in years past. One benefit though was invariably good timekeeping. Behind the engine in the loading dock is what is an interesting vehicle, a former GWR 'Monster' van which had been parked in the same position for many years. Notice also in both this and the preceding image the painting of the station, standard Western Region 'chocolate and cream' albeit somewhat faded having replaced GWR 'light and dark stone'. Finally we see the same engine leaving southbound. Notice also the crew have opened the cab spectacle to encourage some through draught when moving. *All Mark B Warburton courtesy Mrs Margaret Warburton*

Reported by David Bartholomew as the last (almost) original MSWJ signal in use: the down starting signal at Cricklade. (With due allowance for the slightly bent finial.) The point of note is the balance weight high up on the post. The arm, though is not original – as first provided this would have had a single red spectacle only - and is instead a standard LSWR fitting carrying the inscription of 'W R Sykes' who were also the suppliers of much of the signalling equipment used by the LSWR. In the background is the yard weighbridge hut. The signal arm itself was later saved for display at STEAM museum Swindon. *Mark B Warburton courtesy Mrs Margaret Warburton*

The junction at Rushey Platt looking north in 1934. The lines to the left form a passing loop for trains on the MSWJ whilst to the right is the original SMA route from Swindon Town to the GWR. The building on the right – did it ever have a passenger canopy? – is the former station building which was closed to passengers as far back as 1905. Strictly unofficially and for some time afterwards, trains could be persuaded to stop if required. Behind the building it is also just possible to catch a glimpse of wagons in what was Rushey Platt goods yard siding – later serving an expansive timber yard. On the 'main line' the platforms have all but been demolished, these had ceased to be used after October 1905. The signal box seen existed from 1917 – what the arrangements were before this is not clear, and is in the distinctive styling of the LSWR as indeed were other boxes at Swindon Town, Grafton South Junction, Ludgershall, Perham and Tidworth. Recorded in 1934 some years after its last public use, a number of oil lamps are sill visible and which served to illuminate the position of the single line pick up and set down posts. *LGRP*

LENGTH OF LOOPS AT SINGLE LINE STATIONS.

	Length of Loop.	Distance available for crossing.	Number of Bogie Coaches.	Number of Wagons.	Number of Bogie Coaches with No. 1 Class Engine.	Number of Wagons with No. 1 Class Engine.
Cerney	1,490 feet	960 feet	19	48	18	45
Cricklade	1,490 „	910 „	18	45	17	42
Rushey Platt	1,380 „	911 „	18	45	17	42
Chiseldon	1,196 „	810 „	16	40	15	38
Ogbourne	1,246 „	770 „	15	38	14	35
Redposts Junction	1,479 „	915 „	18	45	17	42

RUNAWAY CATCH POINTS.

STATION.	Distance from Signal Box.	Up or Down Road.	Gradient at Catch Points.
Ludgershall for Tidworth Branch	417 yards South of Perham Box	Up	1 in 95
Foss Cross	707 yards South	Up	1 in 107
Chedworth	558 „ „	Up	1 in 1,015

Length of Chedworth Tunnel, 495 Yards.
„ „ Marlborough „ 647 „

The original station at Rushey Platt with a train from Cheltenham on the higher section just exchanging the token in order to continue to Swindon Town. Note the evidence of bricked up doors on the platform side of the original building. Considering the residential and commercial development that has occurred in the area over the years it is hard to imagine that for decades this location was a source of local milk traffic conveyed by train. Notice the single line pick up and set down posts on both lines – the signalman here would likely have to do some walking during his shift. *Lens of Sutton*

The interior of Rushey Platt signal box in 1934: LSWR structure – LSWR lever frame but GWR instruments. These include – to the signalman's right: a No 9 key token instrument for the single line section to Cricklade, and on the shelf (L to R): lamp/signal repeater – Spagnoletti pegging block instrument for trains from Rushey Platt to the GWR main line at what was Swindon Junction – block bell to Swindon Junction – Spagnoletti receiving instrument for trains to Rushey Platt from Swindon Junction – occupation key instrument (one of two in the box) for the use of the ganger in connection with the Motor Economic System of Maintenance - block bell from Cricklade – lamp/signal repeater. At the opposite end of the blockshelf would have been a block bell from Swindon town 'A' and standing on the floor another token instrument for the single line to and from Swindon Town. On the side of the cupboard supporting the token instrument are four cast metal 'reminder' collars used when necessary to prevent a lever being pulled or restored – more usually they were likely used as egg-cups. Signalman Fred Adams is on duty and is using a signalman's duster in exactly the way prescribed so as not to tarnish the tops of the polished levers.

Midland and South Western Junction Railway.

SIGNAL BOXES

Name of Signal Box.		Times during which Boxes are closed.						Monday Mornings
		Week days		Saturday Nights	Sundays.			
		From	To	From.	From.	To.		Opened at
Dowdeswell	..	11·50 p.m.	4·20 a.m. (3·50 a.m. Sats.)	11·50 p.m.	Closed			4·20 a.m.
Withington	..	6·50 a.m.	7·50 a.m.					
		3·30 p.m.	10·0 a.m.	3·30 p.m.	Closed			10·0 a.m.
Chedworth	.	12 no·n	1·30 p.m.					
		Opened only when specially required						
Foss Cross	..	8·0 a.m.	9·0 a.m.	8·0 p.m.	Closed			9·0 a.m.
Cirencester	..	11·30 p.m.	4·30 a.m. (4·0 a.m. Sats)	11·30 p.m.	Closed			4·30 a.m.
Cerney	..	6·50 a.m.	7·50 a.m.					
		11·0 p.m.	4·50 a.m. (4·20 a.m. Sats.)	11·0 p.m.	Closed			4·50 a.m.
Cricklade	..	6·30 a.m.	8·30 a.m.					
		10·55 p.m	5·0 a.m. (4·30 a.m. Sats.)	10·55 p.m.		3·40 p.m.		5·0 a.m.
Rushey Platt	..	6·40 a.m.	8·40 a.m.		5·30 p.m.	3·30 p.m.		5·0 a.m.
		10·45 p.m	5·15 a.m. (4·45 a.m. Sats)	10·45 p.m.				
Swindon	..	6·0 a.m.	8·0 a.m.		5·45 p.m.			5·15 a.m.
		8·45 p.m.	9·45 a.m.					
		11·0 p.m.	5·30 a.m. (5·0 a.m. Sats)	11·0 p.m.	6·10 p.m.	2·15 p.m.		
					9·45 p.m.	9·10 p.m.		5·30 a.m.
Chiseldon	..	11·0 p.m.	5 45 a m (5·15 a.m. Sa s)	11·0 p.m.	6·15 p.m.	2·0 p.m.		
					9 30 p m	9·0 p.m.		5·48 a.m.
Ogbourne	..	10·40 p.m	5·55 a.m. (5·25 a.m. Sats.)	10·40 p.m.	6·30 p.m.	1·45 p.m. 8·50 p.m.		5·55 a.m
		6·50 a.m	8·50 a.m.		9·10 p.m	1·10 p.m		
Marlborough	..	10·30 p.m.	6·0 a.m. (5·40 a.m. Sats.)	10·30 p.m	3·30 p.m.	5·0 p.m.		6·0 a.m.
		7·0 a.m.	8·0 a.m.		9·15 p m			
Savernake	..	10·15 p.m.	8·30 a.m.	10·15 p m	7·0 p.m.	6·0 p.m.		8·30 a.m.
Grafton	..	9·30 p.m.	8·15 a.m.	9·30 p.m.	Closed			8·15 a.m.
Collingbourne	..	6·30 p.m.	8·0 a.m.	6·30 p.m.	Closed			8·0 a.m.
Ludgershall	..	10 30 p.m.	6·10 a.m. (3·50 a.m Sats)	10·30 p.m	1·45 p m	1·0 p.m. 5·0 p.m.		6·10 a.m.
					9·8 p.m.			
Perham	..	10·20 p.m	7·20 a.m.	10·20 p m	9·0 p.m.	8·10 p.m.		7·20 a.m.
Tidworth	..	10·15 p.m.	7·70 a.m.	10·15 p m	9·0 p.m	8·10 p.m.		7·20 a.m.
Weyhill	..	11·0 p.m.	6·50 a.m.	11·0 p.m		12·50 p.m.		
		4·0 p m.	5·0 p.m.		1·20 p.m	5·40 p.m		
					8·30 p m			6·50 a m.

(19)

A very early view of Swindon Town, possibly on the first day of service. Note the engine shed in the distant which is referred to later. At this time there were just two platform faces and no footbridge, access between the platforms being by means of the board crossing, the layout being altered to that seen in the other views c1905. The original 'A' signal box is also visible on the left. On the roof of the first carriage a man is stood whose purpose it was to either place or remove an oil lamp for the benefit of passengers within that compartment. The track has also been ballasted above sleeper level and as was common practice at this time. The general belief was that this was deemed necessary for two purposes, firstly to maintain stability, and secondly if a horse was used for shunting it was easier for the animal to walk on a continuous stone surface rather than alternate stone and timber. The signal seen from the rear is likely to have had a single red aspect only, a white light then standard practice to indicate the 'off'. *George Lait*

Another of the former MSWJ Beyer-Peacock 0-6-0s as rebuilt by Swindon, possibly No 1011, and seen here between Rushey Platt and Swindon Town. Of the engines of this type inherited by the GWR from the MSWJ, the first was withdrawn in December 1934 and the last in March 1938. *LGRP*

Swindon Town was the administrative headquarters of the line during its independent days. The main office is the building on the right and where Sam Fay served (ruled perhaps might be a better description) as General Manager from 1892 through to 1899. Under Fay's leadership the M&G was built whilst receipts increased by 63% against a rise in expenses for the same period of just 15%. The railway was thus placed on a sound economic footing ready for the start of the new century and would continue to hold its own right through until its forced takeover by the GWR. Post grouping the building remained in railway ownership and ended its days as the offices of the local Signalling and Telegraph department. It still stands today now in private commercial use one unusual feature of which being that inside the building the floors are supported on actual rails which are visible in the ceilings so making it extremely sturdy indeed.

Right **On 9th May 1953 the Gloucestershire Railway Society organised a tour entitled an 'MSWJ Outing' from Gloucester down the MSWJ to Andover and returning via Swindon Town, Rushey Platt, Swindon Junction and Stroud. Motive power was one of the final three ex MSWJ engines in service No 1336, hauling three coaches. The special is seen here on the outward run at Swindon Town around 3.15 pm and where there was a five minute stop. (Sister engine No 1335 had been used for a special working over the Shipston-on-Stour branch in August 1952 but was withdrawn the following month.)** *G S Lloyd*

Right **The exterior approach to Swindon Town for passengers and also to the goods yard.** *R Blencowe*

Left **A general view of Swindon Town looking north on 5th August 1961 taken from the footbridge linking the platforms. The pannier tank is at the head of what is probably a Swindon Town – Swindon Junction shuttle although not due to depart until the railwaymen have concluded their conversation! Again lack of revenue earning traffic is apparent. On the left is the turntable, actually the second at the station as until 1905 a two road engine shed and turntable had been provided at the opposite end of the site. There were three platform faces here, that on the left serving as an up loop.** *Mark B Warburton courtesy Mrs Margaret Warburton.*

Left **The companion view to that previously seen with the engine number, 4697, now visible. Originally the double track had extended under the bridge terminating in a headhunt but in more recent times the need to support the bridge on either side had seen the layout altered with the single line slewed to pass through in the middle. Notice the white diamond indicating that track circuiting on that particular set of rails.** *Mark B Warburton courtesy Mrs Margaret Warburton.*

The same engine, No 4697 as seen previous but this time standing 'light' in the up loop whilst a Cheltenham service is taking water at the main platform. Two eras of Great Western signal are visible here, that on the left having a wooden post whilst that immediately behind the water crane is of tubular construction. It is difficult to state categorically when the changeover took place but tubular posts were certainly being used by 1942.

Above **Likely the same train recorded earlier but here seen entering the station from the south. As elsewhere the Western Region paint is beginning to fade whilst the sidings are clearly overgrown, all indicative of a run-down railway. The MSWJ though would not be a victim of Dr Beeching, it had closed before he had taken charge, instead it has the ominous distinction of being the first major closure instigated by the Western Region, regretfully many more would follow. Behind the train the extensive goods shed is visible.** *Mark B Warburton courtesy Mrs Margaret Warburton.*

Right **And so on south to Chiseldon and where on 10th March 1953, No 6323 was photographed leaving the station with the 1023 Cheltenham to Andover. The plethora of signals here was, strange as it may seem, in fact an economy measure instigated in 1952. Rather than single the track through the station, it was instead signalled so that the box might be switched in or our out of circuit as required. Hence, the provision of the bracket signal, the right hand arm of which would only be pulled off when working 'long section' in which case all trains would use the down platform. A similar arrangement was provided at the same time at neighbouring Ogbourne.** *J F Russell-Smith*

Left **The Chiseldon station master was provided with accommodation in the form of this thatched cottage. As can be seen it stood immediately alongside the railway at the north, or Swindon end, of the site***.**

Left **A little over one mile south of Chiseldon was the single platform of Chiseldon Camp Halt located on the south side of the line. A passenger platform was provided here from December 1930 prior to which the same location had seen a siding connection into the Draycott Army Camp between 1915 and 1921. From 1943 until 1950 renewed rail facilities were installed although to a lesser extend than had existed previous.**
Courtesy Mike Barnsley

Right **Busy times at Ogbourne in April 1961 and a grimy pannier meeting its matching twin. No 4697 is arriving from the direction of Marlborough whilst No 8711 waits for the section south to be clear. In the background are the Marlborough Downs. It was across this ridge that both the Marlborough Railway and MSWJ had to cross in order to venture further south. The MR choose to do this with some fearsome gradients as steep as 1 in 58, whilst the MSWJ (through the M&G) opted for an easier passage but one which in consequence involved a tunnel.** *Mark B Warburton courtesy Mrs Margaret Warburton.*

Right **Seen from the south the restricted facilities at both this and most of the intermediate MSWJ stations may be seen although to be fair this was really all that was needed. Passengers would cross the lines here using a board crossing, again a regular feature. Immediately apparent are the various signal wires and point rodding, the latter of an inverted 'U' section likely installed in 1942 and so replacing the original circular rods.** *Mark B Warburton courtesy Mrs Margaret Warburton.*

Local working at Ogbourne in April 1961, five months before closure. No 8711 is on what is a short working – Swindon to Savernake – and is crossing another train heading north, in consequence the signal box here must be switched into circuit. There were just two goods sidings here, visible to the right of the train, the main station building obscured by the coaches. As can also be seen from the bleakness beyond the railway boundary, the term the 'Ogbourne Gap' was well founded, one example being in 1939 when the on-duty signalman was stranded in his box for 40 hours due to snow. The signalbox seen in the background is the 1943 replacement, again to a standard pre-war GWR design but built in 1943. The original structure was on the up platform – hidden by trees in this view - but was retained after its replacement was brought into use, finding a new use as a hut for the permanent way staff. *Mark B Warburton courtesy Mrs Margaret Warburton.*

And so to Marlborough, and as the GWR station had arrived first so we should view this to start with. This is a scene looking towards the GWR (Marlborough Railway) terminus: a single passenger platform having a run-round loop and a single road engine shed at the far end. As can also be seen, a small goods yard was provided at the south end of the station. Through the fence on the right can now be glimpsed the MSWJ route. Notice the lattice post signal home signal. Pure Great Western but slightly unusual, although certainly not unique on the GWR, in that instead of timer lattice metal is used.

We now move east slightly to what was literally the terminus of the then Swindon, Marlborough and Andover railway at Marlborough, the tracks terminating at the end of the platform. This was the situation that existed from July 1881 until February 1883 when after protracted negotiations and difficulties a junction was formed with the GWR line south of the GWR terminus and SMA trains could at last run beyond Marlborough thence via Savernake to reach their own metals again east of the latter station and so on to Andover. Even so it would be another 15 years before the operating difficulties that resulted from this running power arrangement were abolished with the provision of the through M&G line through Savernake Forest. Marlborough station building was not dissimilar to that at Swindon and like its GWR neighbour here, it had provision for goods at the Swindon end of the site.

Below **A fascinating even if slightly damaged image looking from the hill across to the town and including the two stations at Marlborough. The SMA site is to the right with the GWR station and engine shed on the left. Joining the two is a fresh chalk embankment which indicates the course of the connection between the two lines from 1882 onwards. As part way along this chalk (almost in line with the front end of the GWR engine shed) there is a signal post, it is reasonable to assume the connection was then in use. In the foreground is the Marlborough to Savernake road, nowadays the A346, with the toll house at the bottom of the hill.**

G.W.R.

FROM

SUNDAY, OCTOBER 5th,

AND UNTIL FURTHER NOTICE, A

Passenger Service

WILL BE PROVIDED ON

SUNDAYS

ON THE

MARLBOROUGH BRANCH

AS FOLLOWS:—

	P.M.		P.M.
LONDON (Paddington) dep.	4 55	MARLBOROUGH dep.	6 33
READING - - ,,	6 30	SAVERNAKE - arr.	6 45
NEWBURY - - ,,	7 14	SAVERNAKE - - dep.	6 50
SAVERNAKE - - arr.	7 53	NEWBURY - - arr.	7 25
		READING - ,,	8 16
SAVERNAKE - dep.	8 3	LONDON (Paddington) ,,	9 15
MARLBOROUGH arr.	8 15		

For connecting Train Service to and from other Main
Line Stations, see Company's Time Tables.

Paddington Station, London, W.,
October, 1913.

FRANK POTTER,
General Manager.

WYMAN & SONS LTD., Printers, Fetter Lane, London, E.C., and Reading.—13632a.

Left Again looking towards the terminus at the GWR station and with the point of interest being 'Toad' brake van No 35742 branded 'Marlborough'. In the background is the branch engine.

Below left The staff at Marlborough GWR station including the station master in his pillar-box cap and coat. The clerks are likely those wearing the boaters whilst those with caps would be the porters, shunters, signalmen – some roles being combined. Second in from the left may well be one of the branch enginemen with on his right, possibly the GWR Road Motor (bus) conductor as a GWR bus operated from here to the surrounding villages. Other men are likely to be members of the permanent way gang although there would certainly be more than are present. Staff views are always welcome and often a feature of the Edwardian period, a time when Victorian stiffness was beginning to disappear – note the smiling man. The point here is the sheer number of men employed at what was a country terminus, and this did not include a likely similar number of men at the MSWJ station. Post 1924 the GWR station master also took over responsibility for the running of the former MSWJ station, the fate of the MSWJ man not reported.

Right Private owner wagon for Marlborough College with Marlborough MSWJ station shewn as its home site. Livery was purple-brown lettered in white and shaded black. The College had three such wagons numbered 63-65. The Marlborough Gas Company also had their own wagons. Intended for the movement of coal and fitted with grease axle-boxes they would not stay in pristine condition for long.

'Mogul' No 6320 standing 'wrong-road' in the up platform at what is Marlborough Low Level (the suffix was added by the GWR in July 1924) with an engineer's train in April 1960, its position indicating it may possibly be destined for the former High Level site. The sign 'Refreshment Room' may also be noted, this was 'licensed' and served not just passengers (and perhaps staff….) but also formed the 'local' for residents at this end of the town. The GWR Hotels department took over the running of the facility consequent upon the amalgamation, it was managed by Mr Bert Trotman after WW2. Mr Trotman's father, Mark Trotman lived in the High level station building at the time. *I D Beale*

Right **With all passenger traffic diverted to the former MSWJ site from 1933 and Marlborough GWR reduced to goods the High Level location not unnaturally took on a decidedly unkempt appearance. This was the scene in September 1947, the signal box and signals removed although the engine shed, officially closed in July 1933, still stands. Behind the photographer the small yard was still busy although this would reduce over the years and towards the end it was usual to find many of its vehicle occupants were simply kept there in store. Notice too on the extreme right facing the former MSWJ lines, the new GWR signal box, provided in 1933.**

Right **Taken from track level, a view of the connection between the two lines at Marlborough. It is not easy to accurately date the view but at a guess it would be sometime between 1927 and 1933 probably nearer the latter. Signalling is still in place on the High Level line whilst the two coaches appear to be in the post 1927 GW livery. It is unlikely two spare passenger vehicles were kept at Marlborough and so this may also be indicative of the type of train likely to be seen on the GW branch. Realistically the opportunity for much profit on passenger traffic solely between Marlborough and Savernake must have been small although general freight, as is seen from the number of goods wagons around, would have been the more worthwhile commonality.**

Busy times at Marlborough sometime in 1960. In the station, No 31818 is dealing with passengers whilst also waiting for the signal to proceed south. Notice also in the background the pannier tank and coaches. This is waiting its own turn to reach the platform. *M E J Deane courtesy Mrs Margaret Warburton'*

Aware no doubt that the MSWJ was not long for this world, on Saturday 1st April 1961 Mark Warburton spent some time at the station recording what was the highlights of the day workings. Like many country stations that were also crossing places, at Marlborough there might several minutes of frenetic activity followed literally by hours of inaction. We start off though with an arrival from the south, 63xx No 6391 in standard 'grime' livery arriving with a short working from Andover via Savernake Low Level. Since 1933 with the closure of the original GWR branch, the M&G had been converted to operate as two parallel single lines, here of course we are seeing a train the within station limits and on what was the up line through the station but beyond the south end of the loop the right hand line would be used just for services to Savernake Low Level and the left hand line for Savernake High Level trains. By April 1961 the Savernake High Level route had been closed to through traffic since June 1959 although it was physically still in place – hence the two starting signals in the background, and further back, the two home signals for approaching trains. The fireman of No 6391 is placing the carrier and token on the receiving horn of the catcher although it will also be noted that there is no corresponding token to collect for the section north – yet. This is because of what is happening at north end of the station which will be apparent in a moment. On the extreme right is the loading gauge for the Marlborough High Level yard. *Mark B Warburton courtesy Mrs Margaret Warburton.*

Left **No 6391 now reposes in the platform awaiting the next move. A lot of peripheral items of interest here: the goods shed for the Low Level station on the right and a glimpse of the High level engine shed and water tower that were still standing in 1961 nearly 30 years since they were officially closed. The pair of black clad houses are railway dwellings occupied by the station master and one other member of staff, usually the shunter. Two passengers at least appear to be waiting for a down train.** *Mark B Warburton courtesy Mrs Margaret Warburton.*

Below left **Heading back on foot to his previous vantage point, Mark has a view of the approaching down train as it arrived from the direction of Swindon. The short siding on the right had once been used as a loading (and of course unloading) platform for horse-boxes although clearly not for some time. The signalbox, which does not feature in any of this present series, was just out of camera to the right and meaning it may well be the signalman's motorcycle that is conveniently parked on the right. The water column is of interest as there does not appear to have been a similar facility for down trains. It position meant it was likely fed from the supply to the former High Level site. The third train in the background will be discussed shortly.** *Mark B Warburton courtesy Mrs Margaret Warburton.*

The down train has now arrived and with a Southern engine at its head, No 31793, we can conclude it is bound for Southampton. The attitudes of the period are also interesting: passengers using the board crossing without staff supervision and just accepting this as a to be expected way of life. It should be stated that in the timetables Marlborough had for some years dropped the suffix 'Low Level', presumably immediately after the GWR station had closed to passengers back in 1933. The down starting signal has also been lowered and the signalman will no doubt have the token to hand ready to give to the driver of the southbound train as it passes the signal box. The pathway on the left was to and from the staff houses. *Mark B Warburton courtesy Mrs Margaret Warburton.*

No 31793 sets off now on its way to Southampton Terminus, 1 hr 50 minutes and nearly 20 stops away. The 96 mile journey from Cheltenham to the coast would take nearly four hours travelling by the MSWJ, but then how many people wanted to do it anyway? *Mark B Warburton courtesy Mrs Margaret Warburton.*

Moving back to the station, the signalman will have returned the single line token to the relevant instrument sending '2-1' 'Train out of Section' to Ogbourne and when it was acknowledged sending '3-1' 'Is line clear for ordinary passenger train?'. This would be acknowledged by the man at Ogbourne who would also hold down the ringing key on the last beat so allowing a token to be released at Marlborough. The times would be entered into their respective Train Register books by both men after which the Marlborough signalman would set the road and lower the signal before walking up to the train and passing the token to the driver. It was a time consuming and labour intensive system, but it worked. Not just here but on all the single line sections of the MSWJ and indeed on single lines everywhere. Only one token could be taken out of the instruments at either end of a section at any time and provided the driver had possession of this valuable piece of metal – engraved with the names of the stations at either end to which it applied – he was confident he was the only train on the single line. No 6391 about the depart northwards. The shorter signal arm on the bracket: 3 foot length compared with 4 foot, was for the dead-end headshunt where the second train is standing. *Mark B Warburton courtesy Mrs Margaret Warburton.*

Left **Finally in this sequence of Mark's views, we see No 8711 sat at the end of the headshunt awaiting its own turn of duty. Likely this was another short working, Swindon to Savernake perhaps, but which was necessarily sidelined until the crossing move had taken place. Notice the neat and clear condition of the permanent way, again a labour intensive operation but one where pride was taken in the job by the men concerned and who were rewarded with regular prizes in the annual 'Best Kept Length' of permanent way in the district.** *Mark B Warburton courtesy Mrs Margaret Warburton.*

Left **Another short working seen at Marlborough: Swindon to either Savernake or Andover but this time with a 45xx type in charge. The number '50' on the plate referred to the bridge number: all bridges both over and under the line had a reference number (different lines had their own numbering system). Bridge No 50 carried the railway over the A345 Marlborough to Savernake road.**

Our final view of the station here shows another short working, 0-6-0PT No 3763 in charge, and heading south. Tender engines would be used on Andover duties where they could be turned, tank engines might similarly be used or just venture as far as Savernake.

Above **Summer time at Marlborough. A Southern 'Mogul' departing north and about to cross a pannier tank waiting in the spur. In both cases the train are slightly unusual, the Southern engine having just two vehicles – and both GW types in tow – whilst the pannier has a similar set but augmented with a closed van and goods brake van.** *R G Griffiths / SLS*

Right **The rural MSWJ at its best. With storm clouds gathering a pannier tank is seen on the outskirts of Marlborough.** *Roy Denison*

We move south now towards Savernake although first there is the transit of the 648 yard Marlborough tunnel. Opened in June 1898 to operate as a double line between Marlborough, Savernake and beyond, less than three months later temporary single line working was instigated over the up line through the tunnel whilst the down was used for the storage of trains in connection with 'Great Manoeuvres' – military in origin. Restored to double line operation after one week, interlaced single line operation was in use between January and May 1926 and then temporary single line working from July to October 1944. In 1926 and 1944 this was likely to have been for maintenance. The 1944 occasion also saw two temporary signal boxes provided, one at either end of the tunnel and no doubt with token working between the two. Seen here is the north end of the tunnel in April 1914 with a Southampton to Cheltenham working soon to enter Marlborough. *Ken Nunn /LCGB*

The south end, or Savernake end of the tunnel. At the centre of brickwork above the portal was a stone inscribed, 'M & G Rly 1898. This stone was laid by Georgiana Marchioness of Ailesbury'. In this 1950s view the amount of chalk slippage that has occurred over the years is apparent. *T B Sands*

South of the tunnel in August 1943 a ground frame was let into the down line so as to provide a trailing connection of sidings into what was a large ammunition dump well within Savernake Forest. This was in use until August 1950 and received notoriety in 1946 when cases of cartridges intended to be dumped instead exploded without warning resulting in six fatalities and necessitating the subsequent evacuation of residents in the neighbouring village of Cadley, as well as damage to houses here and even as far distant as Marlborough. An aerial film of the aftermath is available at http:// www.britishpathe.com/video/savernake/query/01125700 whilst more detail will also be found in issue of No 22 of 'Great Western Journal'. The view here is post June 1959 looking back towards Marlborough, the one remaining single line now running to Savernake Low Level, the direct route of the M&G which had by-passed the former GWR Berks & Hants line having been removed. *Colin Maggs*

As has been mentioned, in 1933 the GWR rationalised the duplicity that had existed between the former GW Marlborough branch and the MSWJ between Savernake and Marlborough. To do this the line several events took place concurrently. Firstly at the former MSWJ (Savernake High Level) station the double line was terminated at the Marlborough end of the station, the previous down line now being used for all traffic and operating as a single line of rails through Marlborough tunnel all the way to Marlborough. Next the rails of the former GWR Marlborough branch instead of continuing their independent route to Marlborough were now severed at a place referred to as Hat Gate and now slewed into the up line of the M&G at this point, a small amount of earthworks were required at this point. The former up line of the M&G now became a single line between Savernake GW (Low Level) to Marlborough. There was no physical connection between the erstwhile now singled M&G route to Savernake High Level and the route from Savernake Low Level until Marlborough was reached. In this fascinating view the photographer is standing on the truncated remains of the GW Marlborough branch at Hat Gate with his back to Marlborough. Looking forward we see the end of the rusting metals of the Marlborough branch and a fresh chalk embankment indicating the earthworks necessary to connect the line from Savernake Low Level into the former M&G up line. The line of telegraph poles curving away on the far side show the route taken to Savernake High Level whilst to the right the second single line drops away towards Savernake Low Level. This was at a point 25 chains (550 yards) south from the location of ammunition sidings previously mentioned. Of course at the former Marlborough High Level station, the single line in the direction of Savernake was also curtailed and left a shunting neck on what had previously been the single line, 21 chains (462 yards) long in the direction of Savernake. How long the disused rails from the portion of Marlborough branch now severed at both ends remained extant is not known.

Left **Of necessity the railway had to cross the A345 road on its route between Savernake and Marlborough. Two lines merging with each between Savernake and Hat Gate meaning two bridges over the same road. In the first of this small selection we are looking down the hill from Savernake with the M&G girder bridge first followed by the Marlborough Railway structure, taken c1960.** *Marie Dixon*

Below left **In this next view the photographer has parked a mini van on the side of the road facing south to record a down train on part of the original Marlborough Railway route as its coasts down towards Savernake Low Level. (The M&G bridge is behind the camera.) Attempting to park in such a position today would immediately invoke howls of rage from traffic on what is an extremely busy road.** *Marie Dixon*

Right This time it is looking north as another southbound service, likely Southampton bound, coasts down the gradient to Savernake and with steam to spare. Leading the line up of cars is what is a brand new Ford Anglia 'De Luxe' (identifiable as a 'De Luxe' by the chrome grill extending all the way above the bumper). This is followed by an Austin and then a public coach on what was a regular route for such services and of course in direct competition with the railway. Notice the 14 feet 3 inch headroom but only available through the centre of the arch. Following closure both bridges were demolished and the retaining walls also removed. Today it is still possible to identify their position, particularly on the east side of the A345 when heading north, and is marked by the two former railway embankments which come to an abrupt halt just before where the bridges had once stood.

Geographically we move now to Savernake but before doing so it is historically necessary to divert briefly west of Savernake (GW – 'Low Level' station) and refer to the goods siding that had existed at Burbage Wharf a short distance west of Savernake itself. This long lived historic anomaly had started life as an interchange between the Kennet and Avon canal (which runs at a slightly lower level to the railway and to the immediate right of the line of telegraph polls) and the road to Marlborough. Goods for the town being transhipped here from canal barges into cart wagons for the difficult climb over the top of the hill to Marlborough. Come the railway, a siding was provided on the up or London side of the line and was shunted very much on as 'as required' basis. Considering that Savernake (GW) only a very short distance east had its own goods facilities, it is hard to appreciate how the railway facility here lasted as long as it did, but survive in use it did, right through until 1947. Seen here we are looking west along the 'Berks and Hants Extension Railway' towards Pewsey with two rather lonely looking cattle wagons awaiting their next turn of duty. The siding was on a sharp falling gradient away from the main line railway's summit at Savernake and consequently special working instructions stated that shunting and work at the siding must cease when a train was due to pass on the main line. The location of Burbage Wharf is still known today as a turning point for pleasure craft on the restored canal and is marked as being close to where the A345 makes a sharp double bend and narrow bridge immediately after crossing over the railway. *LGRP*

Right We move now to a very early view of Savernake station, probably taken in the 1860s or thereabouts, with broad gauge track and possibly around the time the original Marlborough Railway opened in 1864 – notice the fresh chalk cutting on the right beyond the bridge which corresponds with where the MR bay platform was located. This is looking west with the typical architecture of the B&HER and seemingly before a platform was added for down trains on the left hand side. One can see why with such primitive facilities the Board of Trade inspecting officer, at the time the Marlborough railway came be inspected prior to opening, was critical of the facilities provided.

Right Moving forward some decades we see here what is likely a special train bringing huntsmen and their steeds to Savernake for the hunt. (Although not specifically identified the GWR also had hound vans for the conveyance of the dogs.) A second platform and the associated passenger building has also now been added. Of interest is the wording of the station nameboard. 'For Marlborough' is set to appear very much as an afterthought, whilst there is no evidence to suggest the station had even been specifically called 'Savernake Junction', it was either simple 'Savernake' or post July 1924 'Savernake Low Level'. *The National Archives*

The original Wolfhall Junction signal box 'Cabin' (it would be more strictly accurate if the railway had split the words 'Wolf' and 'Hall') photographed in 1884 – NOT 1883 as been reported elsewhere – see below. (The GWR also had an engine, No 7928 named 'Wolf Hall'.) The signal box was provided at the expense of what was then the SMA company to permit through running from Swindon via the Marlborough branch, through Savernake (GW) station and thence via this junction on to their own metals south towards Andover. But as has been mentioned in the text, it was not a happy relationship and would lead in 1898 to the building of the M&G. This particular box stood on the north side of the Berks and Hants line and was closed in 1899 when the connection between the GWR and what had become the MSWJ ceased to be used at this point. The view shows the contractors engine 'Grosvenor'. This is a Hunslet 0-6-0T known to have built in 1884 as their No 288. Its ownership and use up to the turn of the 20th century are not certain but by c1903 was in the hands of Pauling & Co and was being used on the contract to build the Great Central Railway London extension. *Denis Bird*

Mention has been made earlier of the Kennet and Avon canal which runs east to west connecting into the River Kennet at Reading and also the Wiltshire Avon. At Savernake is the Bruce tunnel, 502 yards long and marking the highest point of the canal over the length of its passage. As later with the M&G railway, the Ailesbury family had played their part in what was an improvement of transport in the area (although they had insisted on a tunnel and not a cutting for the canal at this point) consequently when it was opened a plaque was placed at the eastern end of the tunnel reading, 'The Kennet and Avon Canal Company, Inscribe this TUNNEL with the Name of BRUCE, In Testimony of the Gratitude for the uniform and effectual Support of The Right honourable THOMAS BRUCE EARL of AILESBURY and CHARLES LORD BRUCE his Son through the whole Progress of this great National Work by which a direct communication by Water was opened between the Cities of LONDON and BRISTOL ANNO DOMINI 1810,' The plaque is placed at the east end of the tunnel whilst here we have the west end. The B&HER passes diagonally across the canal tunnel, the signals seen applying to the up main line. The roof of Savernake West signal box may also be seen to the right. *John Bailey*

Left We look now at Savernake GW station, seen west with the junction for the Marlborough line to the right. Savernake West signal box – which roof had just been glimpsed in the previous view - is visible in the distance and with a train due from Marlborough and also a westbound main line service. The photograph was taken in August 1928 at a time when the original Marlborough line was still open. The physical link between the two Marlborough stations had been re-established in 1926 but it is doubtful if any services, passenger or otherwise, worked from here to Marlborough Low Level using it. On the right is the bay platform used for branch trains.
Edward Wallis

Left A few years later some changes are noticeable especially the concrete post for the 'Tilley' lamp. This was a pressurised paraffin vapour lamp which needed to be primed, lit and then pumped to produce a bright illumination. Get it wrong and paraffin would spray in all direction accompanied by much popping and spluttering. The porter would be responsible for preparing the lamps which were attached to a hook at the base of the post and then wound up to the top. Notice the water tank supplying the columns either end of the platform and what looks like a fairly new retaining wall. The counter balance signal arms on left were necessary for advance driver sighting under the foot and road bridges which dissected the platforms. A train is expected on the down main line

A general view of Savernake Low Level this time viewed east and on what appears to be a busy occasion. With only limited genuine local traffic it is likely several of those seen have changed trains here from the Marlborough (or Andover) lines and are awaiting connections to other destinations.
Edward Wallis

Taken from close to the water tank, a 55xx is seen in the Marlborough bay taking water. As mentioned earlier some services, notably on Saturdays, started or ended their journeys from Swindon at Savernake, hence also backing signal seen which would allow the train engine to push the coaches back on to the branch ready to run round, re-couple and then return to the bay – as is seen here. It is also possible that a short train running from Andover to Swindon and having a scheduled lay-over at Savernake might dispose of itself in the bay platform so as to keep the main lines clear. Notice also the platforms were not numbered. The signal is off ready for the train to head back to Marlborough when ready. One of the bridge arches is also needing some support. *R G Griffiths / SLS*

This time it is a pannier tank, No 9740 which is seen arriving at Savernake and is signalled into the up main platform. The train is on the down branch curve, the up branch curve immediate alongside and the track beyond this and closest to the signal box was a refuge siding. There were three signal boxes in close proximity covering the main line in the Savernake area, (five if Burbage Goods and Grafton East were included). The main three were (west to east), Savernake West, Savernake East, and Wolfhall Junction. Hardly strange to relate then that in the late 1930s the GWR sought to consolidate the work of the two Savernake boxes into a single central location. The advent of WW2 however would see an end to the scheme and each would survive until slowly made redundant as closures occurred and MAS came ever closer. The last to remain in operation, and even then only switched in to traffic when required, was Savernake West which was finally taken out of use in November 1978.

A superbly clean tender engine on a 'short' working. This would certainly have originated from Andover and is laying over as it cannot have been that tender first operation would otherwise have applied. 63xx No 6386 is seen at Savernake in 1960 where it will be noted the necessary repairs have now been made to the brick arch. A 5mph speed applied for movements over the pointwork leaving the bay and which is confirmed by the speed limit sign just beyond the bay starting signal. *M E J Deane courtesy Margaret Warburton'*

This time it is the opposite, east end, side of Savernake station with No 5510 arriving from the direction of Andover via Wolfhall Junction and signalled only as far as the junction with the Marlborough branch. The small Savernake (GW station) goods yard is at this end of the station accessed by a trailing connection off the up main. *Mr Williams*

An evening view of Wolfhall Junction signal box dating from the 1960 and which was on the opposite side of the line to the one of the same name seen earlier. Here the topography of the connections between the GWR and MSWJ east of Savernake (GW) are readily seen and explained. First of all the pair of lines coming from bottom left and curving away to the left: this is the 'Berks & Hants' main line, still very much active in 2017 and curving away in the direction of Bedwyn, Hungerford and Newbury. To the right the two lines and the loop on the right, is the original SMA (MSWJ) to Grafton, Ludgershall and Andover. The course of this can be followed for some distance as it makes its way south. Now look at the bridge over the B&H and follow it from left to right. This is the M&G line: to the left it leads to Savernake High Level – which we shall visit shortly – and after crossing the B&H continues south to link in with the SMA at Grafton South Junction, again somewhere we shall visit in a moment. This connection at Wolfhall Junction became redundant in 1898 when the M&G was opened and indeed was closed for a time afterwards. It was reopened for wagon transfers between the two companies in 1900 and for through traffic in 1902. It was also the route used for all north south through trains over the MSWJ for the last couple of years of operation from 1959. If viewed carefully a wagon may be seen at the end of the up loop on the MSWJ line, this may well be a 'cripple' (a vehicle having a defect) removed from a freight train and awaiting attention. Visit the same site today and all that is seen is the pair of main lines and with little evidence of anything else ever having existed.

Retracing our steps slightly this is Savernake (M&G) station – 'High Level' from 1924 with a GWR 'Bulldog' on a down train sometime post 1933. (This is because the passing loop is no longer in existence and all traffic is now using the former up line.) For many years there was a footbridge provided here, hardly warranted when traffic emanating from here would have been considerably less than at Marlborough and where we have seen no such provision was provided. The reason though for this luxury was the insistence of the Marquis of Ailesbury that facilities at the M&G station should be at least equal with that of the GW Savernake station and where a footbridge was provided. Another condition was that a private waiting room for the use of the Marquis (and presumably his guests) was provided, and this took the form of the building on the former down side. How often this obligation was exercised is not known, nor what arrangement might have existed when the down platform ceased to be used for passenger trains. Post 1933 the former down loop was used as a loop siding, but the location was not a block post and instead the single line section was from Marlborough to Grafton South, the former signal box here reclassified as Middle Ground Frame. (Two other ground frames, north and south, all three being released one at a time by the single line token for the section, were provided to operate the points at the ends of the station when required. 'Middle' specifically looked after the points into the loading bay and siding, a glimpse of which can be seen on the extreme left.) The former signal box now carrying a plate reading 'Savernake High Level Middle G.F.'. On the right is the now redundant water tower and column, the latter already devoid of its canvas bag and so meaning water was no longer available for engine purposes. *HMRS*

Left An early view of Savernake (M&G) taken in 1919 five years before the designation 'High Level' would be given. This is looking south from the footbridge unusually perhaps also with a crossover between the up and down lines in the platform. The only reason for this would appear to have been the distance the points were from the signal box which was very much restricted by Board of Trade legislation at the time. *LGRP*

Left Fast forward several decades and Savernake High Level is seen and to be honest starting to appear not a little bit shabby. Notice the gaps in the canopy valance and not just that on the disused down side. This would be in the period leading up to 1959 when the route was closed and severed. As a station, 'High Level' had a life of just 61 years. *T B Sands*

Finally for Savernake (notice the designation 'High Level' does not appear on the nameboard although it was certainly present in the time tables), a scene looking north from a long line of stored brake vans on what was the former down line. The other platform though is certainly still in use. Likely this was taken in the early to mid 1950s, the piles of sleepers indicative of the position of one of the pair of sidings that had once existed behind the station. 'Low Level' station was perhaps 100 or so yards distant and was approached from a connection into the roadway which is seen crossing the line by the over bridge and then continuing at right angles to the railway along the line of trees. The station footbridge is of course long gone. The '260' board indicates a falling gradient of 1 foot in 260 either side of the post.

Returning now to the area beyond both the Savernake stations, we turn to the connection between the two lines leading from the south to Wolfhall Junction. Here again is the Gloucestershire Railway Society tour of 9th May 1953 but seen this time approaching Wolfhall Junction (and the GW main line) from the south. In the background is Grafton South signal box, and with the route of the M&G running behind the engine in a north to south direction. No 1336 was now the very last former MSWJ engine in service and likely too its final visit to what had once been in home metals. It was withdrawn in March 1954 and subsequently scrapped. *J F Russell Smith*

Grafton South Junction. The train is an up freight and has come from the south and is heading for Marlborough taking the M&G line to avoid the GW. Beyond the engine a bracket signal may just be seen with the right hand arm 'off'. This will take the train through Savernake High Level and on to the single line – notice the signalman walking back to his box having just given the token to the crew. The line to the GW and Savernake Low Level diverges to the left ahead of the train and is controlled by the left hand signal on the bracket. To the right the two lines lead to Grafton East (which we shall see in a moment) and provided a direct line for a train to and from the direction of Newbury and Reading to Ludgershall. As if to add confusion and yet another example of how the MSWJ and GWR almost refused to acknowledge each other's existence prior to 1923, this signal box was in MSWJ days named Wolfhall Junction and meaning that there were two boxes of the same name but owned and operated by different companies a little over half a mile apart! Somewhat surprisingly it took the GWR until 1933 a full ten years after absorption to rename the MSWJ box seen here.

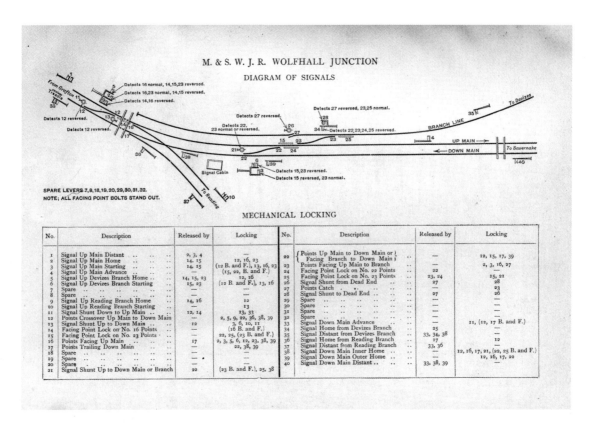

M. & S. W. J. R. WOLFHALL JUNCTION

DIAGRAM OF SIGNALS

MECHANICAL LOCKING

No.	Description	Released by	Locking	No.	Description	Released by	Locking
1	Signal Up Main Distant	2, 3, 4	—	22	Points Up Main to Down Main or Facing Branch to Down Main	..	12, 15, 17, 39
2	Signal Up Main Home	14, 15	12, 16, 23	23	Points Facing Up Main to Branch	—	2, 3, 16, 27
3	Signal Up Main Starting	14, 15	(12 B. and F.), 13, 16, 23	24	Facing Point Lock on No. 22 Points	22	—
4	Signal Up Main Advance	—	(15, 22, B. and F.)	25	Facing Point Lock on No. 23 Points	23, 24	15, 21
5	Signal Up Devizes Branch Home	14, 15, 23	12, 16	26	Signal Shunt from Dead End	27	28
6	Signal Up Devizes Branch Starting	15, 23	(12 B. and F.), 13, 16	27	Points Catch	—	23
7	Spare	—	—	28	Signal Shunt to Dead End	27	26
8	Spare	—	—	29	Spare	—	—
9	Signal Up Reading Branch Home	14, 16	12	30	Spare	—	—
10	Signal Up Reading Branch Starting	—	13	31	Spare	—	—
11	Signal Shunt Down to Up Main	12, 14	13, 33	32	Spare	—	—
12	Points Crossover Up Main to Down Main	—	2, 5, 9, 22, 36, 38, 39	33	Signal Down Main Advance	—	11, (12 17 B. and F.)
13	Signal Shunt Up to Down Main	12	3, 6, 10, 11	34	Signal Home from Devizes Branch	25	—
14	Facing Point Lock on No. 16 Points	—	(16 B. and F.)	35	Signal Distant from Devizes Branch	33, 34, 38	—
15	Facing Point Lock on No. 23 Points	—	22, 25, (23 B. and F.)	36	Signal Home from Reading Branch	17	12
16	Points Facing Up Main	17	2, 3, 5, 6, 12, 23, 38, 39	37	Signal Distant from Reading Branch	33, 36	—
17	Points Trailing Down Main	—	22, 38, 39	38	Signal Down Main Inner Home	—	12, 16, 17, 21, (22, 25 B. and F.)
18	Spare	—	—	39	Signal Down Main Outer Home	—	12, 16, 17, 22
19	Spare	—.	—	40	Signal Down Main Distant	33, 38, 39	—
20	Spare	—	—				
21	Signal Shunt Up to Down Main or Branch	22	(23 B. and F.), 25, 38				

The signal box diagram for the MSWJ Wolfhall Junction signal box, that seen in the last view and which was renamed Grafton South in 1933. This is from the period 1898-1933 (possibly 1905) and shows the main line as that running from left to right (from Grafton MSWJ station to Savernake MSWJ [later 'High Level'] station). The lines shown as 'To Reading' lead to Grafton East, whilst the 'To Devizes' label refers to the connection with the GWR at their own Wolfhall Junction and so on to Savernake (Low Level). All very confusing! The various locking criteria explain that by having a particular lever 'reversed' – meaning pulled across in the frame – other levers are locked and unable to be moved. The purpose of this was to prevent conflicting movements. As an example, signal No 6, (note its position on the opposite side of the track to assist in sighting by the driver of an approaching train), will when pulled lock crossover No 12, the associated disc No 13 and turnout 16. In order to release signal No 6 crossover 23 would have to be pulled first and then locked by lever 15. Neither No 15 nor No 23 could be altered until first signal No 6 was put back to 'danger'. The principle however was that a signal could always be restored to danger at any time if was necessary to attract the attention of the train crew, but by doing so this would also leave the respective lock and then crossover potentially free to be moved, perhaps even in front of or under the train itself. Note no track circuits are shown and they may not have existed here. The physical position of the signals also altered post 1933.

Right A short freight, likely a pick up goods, heading south on the M&G route south of Savernake High level and passing over the B&H main line. The engine is a BR Class 2 2-6-2T, BR standard types certainly seen on both passenger and freight workings in the final years. Immediately to the right is the connection from Grafton South Junction up to Wolfhall (GWR) junction. It was the condition of the bridge over which the train is passing that lead to the closure of the M&G route in June 1959, traffic and in consequence receipts not considered viable to justify repairs.

Right Around the same time this local passenger working arrived from Grafton South heading for Savernake Low Level. The goods train seen in the previous view having traversed the lines on top of the embankment. In the background the bridge carries both this connection and the M&G over the Kennet and Avon canal.

Above No 5957 'Hutton Hall' on a down local B&H train swinging past Grafton East and heading west. This could well be a Reading to Bristol, via Devizes, working. On the right and in the middle of the 'four foot' is a GWR ATC ramp for trains coming off the line from Grafton South. The siding behind the signal box was for stabling a banking engine if required and was also the nearest railhead for coal destined for the canal pumping engines at nearby Crofton.

Above left Another view of Grafton South and with the signal off for a train to head south – either from Wolfhall or the direction of Savernake High Level. Again the line to and Grafton East are visible but from their covering of rust not having seen much use recently.

Left And so to Grafton East – 'Grafton Curve Signal Box' until renamed in 1933. Confirming what has been stated earlier, the connection here allowed trains to run from the GWR B&H main line to and from Reading. The two lines on the right are the B&H main line heading west towards Savernake Low Level, Pewsey and beyond. Those to the left go to Grafton South. Again the canal will be seen passing under the connecting line. *Norman Simmons*

Left In May 1957 the curve from Grafton South to Grafton East was taken out of use (the bank engine siding at the latter had been removed the previous year). It was likely lifted soon after leaving just the duty signalman's access across the trackbed. At the same time several levers within both controlling signal boxes would have been rendered redundant. The view is looking on to the former chord from the south and was taken from a passing train in July 1960. (Grafton East signal box reminding in use until November 1964 although its relevance to any MSWJ line workings was now nil. One fascinating survivor from the period is a signal box train register from Grafton South example pages from which may be viewed at http://pewseyvalerailwaysociety.webplus.net/graftonsouth.html) *R Montgomery*

Below left Another short freight heading south on the M&G route and about to cross over the B&H likely on its way to Andover.

Right In June 1959 engineers decreed the bridge carrying the former M&G line over the B&H between Grafton South and Savernake High Level was unfit for traffic, it was removed soon afterwards. The route of the M&G north from Grafton South was thus severed just before the bridge and the line closed to all traffic through Savernake High Level as far as Marlborough. Here the abutments of the bridge are all that remain although access to the southern section of the MSWJ via Wolfhall Junction was of course still possible – these are the lines seen on the right. On the main line Wolfhall Junction up advanced starting signal and the Grafton East up distant have both been cleared for a train heading east towards Reading.

Right Seen from the south, the connection to Wolfhall Junction from Grafton South heads to the left whilst the now redundant stub of the M&G is to the right. Notice too the wartime tank traps, the Kennet and Avon canal was seen almost as a last line of defence against invasion in 1940 running as in does, in connection with the River Thames, east to west and so forming a water barrier to an invading army. This also explains why so many pill-boxes and the like were situated along the length of the waterway.
Colin Maggs

INTERLUDE- STAFF AND ENGINEERING

Locating staff views is one of the pleasures of any research, the posed view at Marlborough GW has already been seen, but here we have three images of individuals all going about their daily tasks, unseen by most but which were an essential part of safe railway operation.

Left First is Charlie Tilley (no known connection with the platform lamp of the same name) with various signal lamps on a special carrying yoke. The lampman's duties were vital to safe working. Semaphore signals had oil lamps to illuminate the glass spectacle at the end of the signal arm and so give a red or green (sometimes yellow of course dependent upon the actual signal) indication to the driver at night. This was achieved using a paraffin filled lamp, consisting a circular reservoir, casing and a wick. A curved and polished plate was slid behind the wick to reflect the flame forward and which was further magnified by a 'bulls-eye' lens in the lamp housing. The capacity of most lamps was just a single day, during which time they would burn continuously. ('Long burning' lamps were provided at some locations whilst on some very quiet branch lines having just a daytime service, the lamps were not lit for certain months of the year.) Daily then the local porter – at some locations where there were numerous signals a lampman was employed – would attend to each lamp on a rotational basic. Lamps were refilled and wicks trimmed as necessary together with the reflector polished, all this was usually done in the lamp hut near each station. Once smelt the aroma is never forgotten, a paraffin soaked shelf home to several lamps, some refilled, some waiting attention. Surprisingly these huts never seemed to catch fire despite so many staff being regular smokers. Dependent upon the area to be covered the man charged with this task would deal with his patch carrying one or even two sets of lamps. New ones would replace the old with the latter being taken back to the lamp hut for attention. The GWR used a standard lamp housing but that is not to say there was a possible interchange between a GWR signal and those standing on the MSWJ. (One of the reasons standard GWR fittings quickly replaced the former MSWJ lamps.) The same type of lamp would be used to illuminate the position and posts of the token pick-up and set-down posts. Here the location is close to Grafton Junction, in the 'four foot' of course, and somewhere where track circuiting existed – hence the wires either side of the fishplate. Smart shoes, a railway cap – and a necessary head for heights – the latter essential, as apart from when servicing the ground signals a ladder climb would invariably be required. *Gwenda Ellison*

Far left Jim Hunt near to Grafton South. It is not immediately clear from the photograph what Jim's role was on the railway. One is tempted to suggest a member of the permanent way gang, he is perhaps a bit young to be a ganger, and in any case such a man would be expected to have key-hammer and spanner across his shoulder. Possibly the Grafton South signalman? *Gwenda Ellison*

Below This next view is of Jim Hunt and 'Jim' Flippance with a hand propelled p/way trolley believed to be on the up line at Grafton South opposite the signal box. As with the other views in this small series, no date is given. (It appears there is a token set down post in the background.) Regardless of the location, and assuming this is a running line and not a siding, the men would have obtained the permission of the signalmen controlling the section of line before placing their trolley on the line. The structure behind could well be a lamp hut. *Gwenda Ellison*

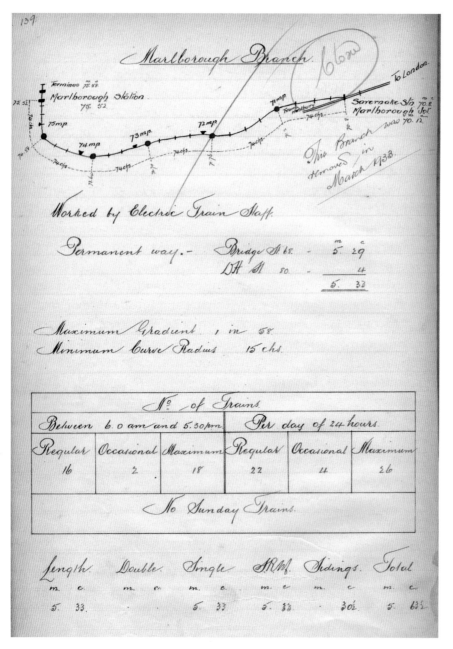

A fortunate find some years ago was an official Paddington register describing the installation of the Economic System of Maintenance on the GWR Marlborough branch in 1910 and then subsequently on the former MSWJ from Cirencester as far south as Marlborough in June 1927. As the name implies, the idea was to effect economy in maintenance relative to the permanent way and which under the old regime required two men to act as lookouts either side of any site of work. Although performing a vital safety role, they were otherwise ineffective in contributing to the actual work. The ESM changed this by allowing the ganger, or man in charge of the work, to take possession of a (brass) key and which when in his charge prevented a single line token from being obtained and so allowing any train to approach. The key was obtained with the permission of the signalmen at either end of the section and unlike a token, could be restored at any one of a number of intermediate key boxes within section and which would then in turn restore the token system to use. Once a train had passed, the ganger could again, with the consent of the signalmen, obtain the occupation key once more safe in the knowledge that he was working in perfect safety. The cost of the installations was offset by the saving in manpower achieved – economy a feature of railway working even in the early years of the 20th century, the fate of any displaced men not reported. So far as the Marlborough branch installation was concerned, one gang of six men now did the work of what had been two gangs of four and with a consequent saving of £109. 4s in 1910 against an initial investment of £122. This in just over one year the scheme would be 'in profit' and save for any occasional extra costs associated with periodic maintenance of the equipment, this saving would continue to accrue in subsequent years. The system continued in operation until the original line closed in 1933. The Paddington file also giving some useful and interesting details of the route, the train service, and the location of the associated intermediate key boxes.

140

No. of Huts provided with Telephones and Occupation key Instruments.   5.

Telephones are fixed at Savernake and Marlborough Stations.

Estimated cost of Installation :-

	£	s.	d.
Telephones and Occupation key Instruments.	80	0.	0.
5 Telephone Huts	7.	10.	0.
1 Velocipede Car Hut.	3.	0.	0
1 Car	7.	10.	0
1 Mechanical Trolley	11.	5.	0
1 Watch	2.	0.	0
1 Suit, oilskins for Ganger.		15.	0
Total £	122.	0.	0

Under Standard Rules this Branch was maintained by :-

	Total No. of men	Wages per annum	No. of men per mile
2 Gangs of 4 men ea.	8	396. 10. 0	1.38
Under new System :-			
1 Gang of 6 men	6.	287. 6. 0	1.04.
Gross saving in men + wages per ann.	2.	109. 4. 0	.34

The Ganger has been provided with a watch and examines his length daily on a Velocipede Inspection Car Mechanical Trolley provided for Gang.

Economic System brought into operation 1st August 1910.

Andoversford Line - Marlborough to Cirencester.

From 19.45 to 45.58 - Line worked by Electric Train Tablet.

Converted to Motor Trolley working

Maximum Gradient - 1 in 75.
Minimum Curve - 6 chains.

Section.	Number of Trains.					
	During 24 hours.			Between 7.0am & 5.0pm		
	Regular.	Occasional.	Maximum	Regular.	Occasional.	Maximum.
1. Marlboro' & Cirencester.	24	4	28	14	4	18.
2. Swindon to Marlboro'.	6		6	6		6.
3. Swindon (GW) to Swindon Town	14		14	8		8
Sunday Trains			11.			

Length of Line under Economic Maintenance:- 26·13 chs

3. line.	Double line.	Single.	Single Running Miles.	Sidings. m. c.	Total. m. c.
0·22	2·22a	23·28½	28·19¼	5·48½	33·68

Estimated cost of Installation:-
Signal Department.   £
   Occupation Key instruments & telephones.   2,665
Engineering Department
   Bicycle Cars Mech. Trolleys Huts etc.   700.
                                                                        _____
                     Amount of Vote £4,653 3,365.*

* The average distance between telephones was extended from 58 chs to about 70 chains. thus effecting a saving in seven boxes and instruments. This with the substitution of telephone boxes for telephone huts effected a saving on the original vote of over £490.

The Signal Engineer advised in Feby 1928 that a saving of £431 had been effected on the estimate through simplifying the system & utilising 2" bore telephone

Under Standard Rules this section of line was maintained by:-
   Nine gangs with a total strength of 40 men - 1·13 mpg

Under the Economic system there will be

   Six gangs with a total strength of 29 men - ·87·4

The Estimated saving in wages due to the introduction of the Economic system of Maintenance is:

        £1,308 per annum.

Gang 167 Marlborough maintains from 19.45 to 20.0 but do not come under the Economic system.

By installing a "loud speaker" in each of the Signal Boxes controlling the occupation Key system the Gangers or other person in charge of the occupation key can communicate with the signalman without surrendering the occupation of the line - or restoring the occupation Key in the instrument.

Gang 133. Swindon is not provided with either Bicycle Car or Mechanical trolley as they only maintain a short length of running line.

Two Keys are provided on the following sections to enable the Gangers of adjoining gangs within a Staff Section to obtain occupation at the same time.
   Ogbourne to Chiseldon -   Swindon A to Rushey Platt
   Rushey Platt to Cricklade -

System introduced between Cirencester & Swindon - 13th June, 1927
   -do-   Swindon & Marlborough 20th June, 1927.
                                      See Papers. 678a/177. K.

The 1927 installation between Cirencester and Swindon and then on the Marlborough was a far larger scheme and would effect a saving of from 40 to 29 men equal to £1,308 pa against an installation cost of £3,365. In both the Marlborough and MSWJ schemes the men in the p/way gangs would still have to walk to the required site of work carrying what equipment they needed. The alternative would be a hand propelled trolley on to which large or heavy items would be loaded. For this to be placed on the track the occupation key would be needed. Once at the site of the work and if the line was required for normal traffic, the trolley was removed from the track and the occupation key restored.

In addition to a hand trolley, under the ESM each ganger was issued with a hand powered 'velocipede' to enable him to inspect his 'length'. (The term 'length' referred to the section of line each gang was responsible for.) The machine might best be described as a bit of bone-shaker but was also cleverly designed so it might be operated by sitting and pulling/pushing on a set of handles. These in turn connected to a basic drive mechanism. 'Gearing' was provided in the form of a further set of handles higher up – the ones being seen to be held in the illustration. A hammer and fishplate spanner might be carried on the cross member. Care had to be taken on steep down gradients and also at turnouts as any slight deviation could easily tip the machine, indeed bruised egos (and other more physical parts of the anatomy) were not uncommon. Notwithstanding the provision of mechanical transport, each ganger was still inspected to walk through the length weekly. Normally of course just one man would use the machine, there being no provision for a passenger. In what is clearly a posed family group, one of the machines is seen, likely in the area of Cirencester. No names for those seen are given although the man standing could likely be a station master. *Corinthian Museum*

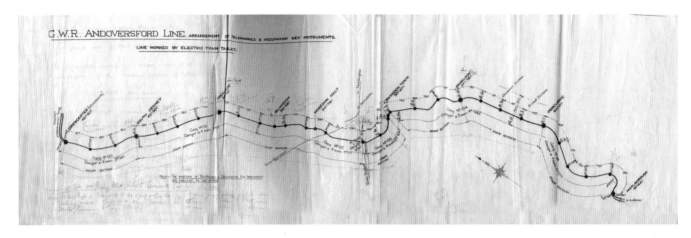

G.W.R. ANDOVERSFORD LINE. ARRANGEMENT OF TELEPHONES & OCCUPATION KEY INSTRUMENTS.

LINE WORKED BY ELECTRIC TRAIN TABLET.

Above **After only about one year in operation, the ESM began to be superseded by the Motor Economic System of Maintenance with that on the MSWJ from Cirencester as far south as Rushey Platt believed to have been the very first in March 1928. (The conversion to MESM was subsequently extended to Marlborough although no date for this is known.) Technology had developed and now the hand propelled trolley and hand operated velocipedes were replaced by motorised versions. Able to cover a greater distance quicker, there were again likely staff savings but this time no details are available. What is provided, however, is a plan showing the installation on the MSWJ. As to why the MSWJ should be chosen as a pioneer is not certain but it is likely the GWR were keen to test matters on a route where traffic was not heavy and any difficulties could be resolved without undue delays being caused. In fact there were none and the MESM went on to be developed and used on countless**

sections of what were basically sections of single line having just with passing loops. Indeed elsewhere several of the ESM systems were subsequently converted to MESM. In only one area on the GWR however – and that was not the MSWJ – was the system ever trialed on a double line. The MSWJ would retain MESM between Cirencester and Marlborough until the end of its life. North of Cirencester and south of Marlborough (post 1933 in the latter case) the single line sections might have similarly be suitable but for whatever reason this was not done.

Right **Ganger Ernest Neale and his daughter Mary proudly posed on the inspection trolley in Cirencester station. Basic illumination consisted of a paraffin lamp – or two. It is not believed any horn was provided for the inspection trolleys. Note also the identification number, 'GW S15'.** *Corinthian Museum*

Below left **The Cirencester ganger on his petrol powered individual inspection trolley although it will be noted there was no provision for another man to be carried. No protection against the elements was provided. The machine was light enough to be manhandled on and off the rails as required although if he was on his own this would be one end at a time. Again the ride was harsh and after various incidents (possibly on the MSWJ but certainly elsewhere) instructions were issued that men be made aware that the machines could become derailed at spring points whilst they must not also be regarded as reliable in operating track circuits.** *Corinthian Museum*

Left **A large motorised trolley capable of seating six men was also provided for each gang. This could also tow a trailer as seen here, although riding on the trailer was not always the safest place to be especially if lengths of rail were also being carried. Here in what is clearly a posed view the gang members, plus perhaps the local Permanent Way inspector are seen on the down line at Cricklade. Behind is another variant of the individual inspection trolleys, this time with a small windscreen. In the background is the tower of St Sampson's church.** *Corinthian Museum*

Left **Back at Cirencester, easily identified by having the works in the background, we have a view of the trolley and this time replete with its portable turntable by which it might be readily moved off the track – at 'home stations' a hut might be provided or at the very least a set of rails at 90° to the running line on which the trolley might be stabled. The engine is believed to have been of 'JAP' manufacture and with the position of the petrol tank also visible. Starting was by means of the handle seen.** *Corinthian Museum*

Finally in relation to trolleys, a much later 'Wickham' type on the up line at Marlborough in BR days. Human comforts had come a long way since 1928. At least one brass occupation key for the area around Rushey Platt survives, this is at the private railway museum of Sir William McAlpine. *R E Toop*

PART 2B - THE ORIGINAL RAILWAY GRAFTON TO WEYHILL INCLUDING THE TIDWORTH BRANCH

Continuing our journey we reach Grafton, 'Grafton and Burbage' until June 1898. This was also the temporary terminus of the line up from Andover from 1882 until the connection was made with the GWR at Wolfhall Junction in 1883. This view is looking south with a train approaching from Collingbourne (we have cheated slightly as it is in fact one of the last day specials – see later). There was a small goods yard at the south end of the site on the up side and which continued in the form of a goods loop behind the goods platform. Behind the camera and to the left there had, until 1956, been a down refuge siding. This was the last remnant of further sidings that had also once served the Dodsdown Brickworks branch, in operation for just eight years from 1902 to 1910. This railway – tramway might be a better term – is known to have operated an outside cylinder 0-6-0T with the name 'A J Keeble'. *Photos from the Fifties*

Past Grafton and we arrive at Collingbourne Kingston Halt three miles further south. This stopping place had been opened by the GWR in 1932, one of numerous local halts throughout the system which purpose was to attempt to tap into local traffic that might otherwise be lost to road competition. Facilities here, as indeed at nearly all halts were basic, a wooden platform and corrugated hut on each platform, and a single lamp for illumination: here it was electric no doubt because of the obvious nearby supply. 'Supervision' was exercised from Collingbourne, and meaning in practice a porter would attend at intervals to ensure all was in order. Otherwise no staff were provided although local passengers might purchase travel tickets from the GWR agent a short distance away on the main road. This view is looking north in 1959 with passengers instructed to use the pathway and road bridge to reach the opposite platforms. *Amyas Crump collection*

Only one and quarter miles on was Collingbourne station where we have a view of the signal box located on the down platform. Again provided by the Gloucester Carriage & Wagon Company it had 16 levers including two spares. Although fixed signals were naturally provided for the up and down running lines, it is interesting to note that there were no ground signals controlling the trailing crossovers between the running lines nor for accessing the loading dock or goods yard. Although unusual this was by no means unique on the MSWJ or indeed elsewhere.

Two miles south of Collingbourne we reach Ludgershall and the junction of the Tidworth branch. In this early view the 'main line' from Collingbourne appears as the second (down) and third (up) lines from the right. The route to Tidworth is that curving off to the left. In the distance is the bridge that carries the Devizes road over the line. Notice on the left what is a troop platform, possibly added when the War Office were developing the area as a military camp and subsequently deemed no longer required when the branch to Tidworth was opened. The view was taken in 1918 with the main line doubled whilst the engine shed – centre left – was added in 1903 present. Here was also a turntable. Centre right is the goods shed. The signals seen are the respective home signals for Ludgershall from both Collingbourne and Tidworth. Unfortunately it is not possibly to identify the individual locomotive although it is likely one of the pair of Dubbs built 0-6-0 tank engines either No 13 or 14, one of which was semi-permanently based at Andover for working the Tidworth branch. Both would pass into GWR hands and lasted until mid 1926.

Half a century or so later and No 7810 'Draycott Manor' has charge of a train bound for Andover at least and likely Southampton. The days of the MSWJ engines and also the GWR 'Duke' and 'Bulldog' classes have come and gone and this somewhat larger engine should have had little trouble with its four coach load. The train is seen in an almost identical location to the previous view, the line to Tidworth to the left and straight ahead to/and from Collingbourne. The road bridge also shows up better in the background. *D W Winkworth*

The largest LSWR 'centre-pillar' design signal box on the line at Ludgershall – following the closure of Rushey Platt also the largest station so far as number of platforms and bays was concerned. The image here was likely taken in the final years and with the unusual but not unique feature of the MSWJ in that the LSWR style signal boxes had GWR style cast name plates – cast name plates for the signal boxes on the whole line were ordered in 1923/4. To the immediate right is the bay platform used for trains to Tidworth whilst that seen in the foreground is the up main platform. Access to the signal box was by a set of external steps at the south end. The station here possessed considerably wide platforms all intended to ease the en-training and de-training of troops and indeed for many years cavalry and other horses. Passenger facilities were principally concentrated on the down side with only a basic shelter – just visible in the background – on the up platform. *Amyas Crump and Alan Jarvis*

Above **Looking south at Ludgershall with the down bay platform in use. Years earlier horses would have been loaded and troops entrained here The light film of rust on the rails had probably been acquired overnight even though the railway was still in use at this time.**

Right above **We move now the period around the start of the 20th century and the building of the branch from Ludgershall to Tidworth and just two and half miles in length. Seen here is deep cutting though the chalk of Tidworth Down. Construction was undertaken by the War department who would have sub-contracted out, possibly to the firm of Henry Lovatt. It is likely local labour was used although no doubt some men also came from outside for concurrent with the railway construction work was also progressing with Tidworth barracks and it is unlikely the area alone could have supplied all the necessary men.**

Right **Contractors trains likely at Ludgershall – as the chalk is not freshly cut. It is not certain if those on board are all actually navvies might this even have been a celebratory working at the completion of the work? Construction workers from outside who were employed on building both the railway and the barracks, were housed at a temporary labour camp known as Brimstone Bottom near Ludgershall.**
David Foster-Smith

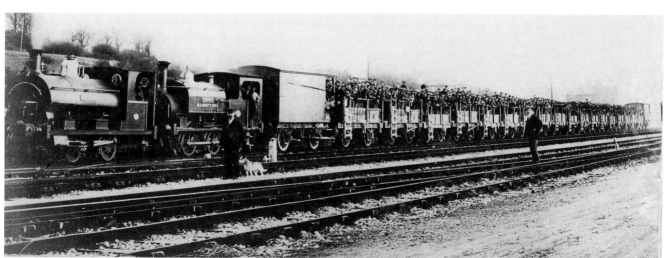

Right Outside of station limits at Ludgershall and Tidworth, the branch was just a single line. This is looking towards Ludgershall with the lower arm the Tidworth advanced starting signal and the taller arm the outer home signal. Both were controlled from Tidworth signal box which was located jest off the east end of the troop platform. *J D Beale*

Left above The completed terminus at Tidworth with No 13 entering from Ludgershall in 1913. It has been mentioned before but it is still worth repeating: receipts from this station alone surpassed the combined total of all the other MSWJ stations and due solely to the impact of the army. Facilities for public passenger services were restricted to the one platform, an 800 feet platform on the opposite side used for troop traffic. In addition there were numerous siding and loading faculties north of the site. Seen here is a local working, any revenue from non-military traffic an added bonus.

Left below Amongst the sidings mentioned was a single line of rails that headed into Lucknow Barracks at Tidworth. From the photograph the track here is light section laid on half-round timbers. Clearly a steep gradient was also involved. It is likely this line was used for supplying stores. *J Williams*

Approaching Ludgershall from Tidworth, the single line became double at Perham Down about two miles from the terminus. To control the connection, plus a level crossing and various sidings, a signal box again in LSWR style, was provided. This took on a new significance when various new sidings and connections were provided in WW2. This view was taken in 1920 with three local members of staff in view, plus a glimpse at some horticultural endeavours plus of course 'Fido'.

As referred to above, public passenger services afforded scant revenue and it was no surprise when British Railways announced the withdrawal of public passenger services from 19th September 1955. It was an inevitability that would see the same occurrence happening on the remainder of the former MSWJ six years later. On the last day Ivatt Class 2, No 41305 is seen arriving at the terminus and then having run-around is recoupled ready for the return working. As can be seen the troop loading platform has a number of half-tracks loaded.
Rev D Littlefair

The final passenger working was hauled by 2-6-0 No 5326 seen in the bay at Ludgershall prior to departure: arrived at Tidworth and then ready for the final departure. A passenger with a suitcase shows the railway still had some purpose whilst the look on the faces of the two women seems to almost express surprise at the wreath being carried. A few are likely making a final journey although in the main the occasion passed without any great fanfare. Following public closure the signal box was quickly reduced in status to that of a ground frame and all associated signalling removed. Public goods ceased to be handled after November 1955 although military traffic continued until as late as November 1963, officially four months after the branch had been officially closed. The bay platform at Ludgershall was also taken out of use after November 1955. The closure of the line appears not to have generated any mention in the railway periodicals of the time and unlike what would occur in 1961, no enthusiast specials are reported to have run.

Up to 1943, the railway south of Ludgershall for the final few miles through Weyhill to Red Post and Andover had been single line. Consequent upon wartime needs it was doubled in 1943 and remained as such until August 1960 when rationalisation again took place. This increase in capacity was one of countless new works undertaken by the GWR at the behest of the Government in WW2 examples of which were recorded by the GWR official photographer and reported as 'Progress'. Here we see three examples near Weyhill with a cutting being opened out, the garden of what is likely a cottage guarding an occupation crossing being cut back, and finally at Weyhill itself in connection with the laying of the single line. It is believed this work was carried out without the necessity to curtail services except for very short periods.
GWR

INDEX